"Delve into the minds of visionary leaders who understand that to recruit and retain great talent, you have to care with consistency. In Catalysts of Culture, Julie Ann Sullivan has brought 14 creative thinkers to your doorstep to develop your own unique significant employee experience."

Ken Blanchard Co-Author of the One Minute Manager and Servant Leadership in Action

"If you are looking for proven cultural philosophies to transform your organization, Julie Ann Sullivan, has done the research for you. Catalysts of Culture brings you a wide variety of industries and personalities with one common denominator...success."

Marshall Goldsmith, recognized by Thinkers50, Fast Company, INC Magazine & Global Gurus as the World's Leading Executive Coach

CATALYSTS

OF CULTURE

Julie Ann Sullivan

MOtivational PRESS®
LEADERS IN GLOBAL PUBLISHING

Published by Motivational Press, Inc.
1777 Aurora Road
Melbourne, Florida, 32935
www.MotivationalPress.com

Manufactured in the United States of America.

ISBN: 978-1-62865-644-2

CONTENTS

FOREWORD

TODAY'S LEADERS, ENTREPRENEURS, and business owners know they need to engage, connect with, listen to, and include their people (as well as their customers, clients, partners, vendors, and communities) in the conversations surrounding the business. They must make them feel that their goals and the goals of the business and its leaders are aligned—because they are, and not just on paper in the words of their corporate values. That's how you create a winning culture.

Leaders know that the workplace has changed – employees are more than the 9-to-5 grind and want more than a paycheck. They want a place where they can feel engaged, appreciated, and valued. 'Culture' used to be a buzz word used to describe companies like Apple, Google or any other 'trendy' Silicon Valley-based start-up with a large millennial workforce. However, as millennials now compose the largest workforce in the country, companies have made the word 'culture' go from a buzz word to run of the mill.

The importance of having a winning culture can't be overstated enough. A company's culture is reflected on their values, their employees and the all-around environment in which they operate. It's the people that bring the culture to life – every day heroes that transform and elevate their game at every turn.

Julie Ann's book provides readers with real-life experiences of true and tested leaders from a wide variety of industries. Leaders who are great listeners, are open to new ideas, are constantly learning and create a positive and inclusive overall experience for the entire team, where diversity of thought is the order of the day. If you're looking to begin to create, or continue to cultivate, a cohesive team, this book will explore different ways where everyone on the team can shine and bring their collective superpowers to the table. Just like the Avengers, alone they're powerful, but collectively, they're invincible. Assemble your team and watch their superpowers explode into greatness.

Jeffrey Hayzlett -- Primetime TV & Podcast Host, Speaker, Author and Part-Time Cowboy

LET'S GET STARTED

"Only in community do we have the resources to help everyone succeed."
—Julie Ann Sullivan

SEVERAL YEARS AGO, I decided to start a podcast. My original podcast was called Mere Mortals Unite. The podcast centered on superpowers that everyone has, but may have lost, or given away, or never even known that they had. I've always been a firm believer that many of us have a lot more power than we think, and we tend to keep it uncultivated and hidden, even from ourselves. My guests would talk about their own superpower, but it had to be one everyone could possess. They ranged from authenticity to being a risk taker. Each guest would give the listener ideas on how they could enhance this superpower within themselves.

As my work grew with employee engagement and business work environments, I had my own ideas and experiences about what it took to create a great culture. Of course, I wanted to validate that, so I created a podcast series, Businesses that Care. I went out and found leaders who understood that a thriving internal culture had its benefits. More importantly, they were willing to do the necessary work to build and sustain it. The research has grown over the years and has shown that high levels of employee engagement directly affects the bottom line in a multitude of ways. Companies experienced higher profit, higher retention rates, increased productivity and enhanced problem solving.

It takes companies less time to recruit great talent when their culture reputation precedes them. Great cultures establish an environment where the workforce is allowed to grow with the tools and skills necessary to collaborate on a very high level. This establishes a workplace where creativity and problem solving thrives. Another bonus of this type of culture is not worrying about other people stealing your talent. And possibly most important, the relationships the workforce has built with each other, and your clients and customers, have a lasting effect. Customer loyalty means repeat business and referrals.

I am in awe of the leaders I have had the privilege of interviewing and building relationships with. I have talked to companies from diverse industries, including real estate, media, moving, tire companies, landscaping and banking. Some businesses are household names, like FASTSIGNS and WD-40 and some will surprise you, like the University of Mississippi, or RNR Tire Express. I've talked to men and women from all across the United States, Scotland, and Australia…so far. Ultimately, I picked 14 of these amazing visionaries for you to experience and utilize their proven ideas to create excellence. After interviewing these distinct companies, I found that each of these visionary leaders had four attributes that they all possessed.

The first of those attributes was that they were great listeners. Communication was important to them, but where they stood out the most was in the area of being present. Here is what that means; when they had a conversation with you, they made themselves available. Not just in time, but in mind. They did not live in a high castle with four gatekeepers, they were among the very people who carried out the purpose of the company. They were conscientious about where and when they had conversations, depending on the need of the individual and the situation. They learned how to talk less and concentrate more on the person that was speaking. As human beings, we have been given two ears and one mouth. I think there's a reason for that.

The second attribute, which goes right along with the first, is that they were open to new ideas. They were open to new ideas, even if they were different from anything they had ever thought of. New ideas falling on closed ears stifles creativity and what could be extremely beneficial to your organization. New ideas don't necessarily come as ideas for a new product or service. It might be a new idea about how to perform a process in your company more efficiently. It might be reporting something that isn't working well. Leaders, who truly listen and are open to new ideas, build an environment where people feel they won't be ignored or punished for coming forward. These leaders are keenly aware of the possibilities.

The third attribute has to do with continuous learning, not only for themselves, but also for their entire workforce. The women and men that I spoke with are constantly reading books and articles, going back to school or showing up for seminars. They involve themselves with mentors, coaching, mastermind groups and organizations that help their company grow. While they were doing this, they made sure everyone in their workforce had the same opportunity. They made it a priority that the people who drive their business had the tools and development that was necessary to do their job at their full potential. Many include skills, like money management, healthy habits and strategic thinking, to serve their workforce holistically. You can see how these three attributes tie together. If you're listening and listening to new ideas, you're learning.

The fourth attribute is creating a safe environment. The kind of safe environment I'm talking about is one in which people can have a difference of opinion. My guests all showed a willingness to make sure that everyone had the skills they need to take a difficult conversation and come to a solution, as opposed to a confrontation. The importance of having a safe place shows up in many different scenarios. It may be when someone feels able to step-up and say, "There is a problem with how we are making this product. It's not safe." When you don't have that kind of environment, you have multimillion-dollar recalls or lawsuits. A safe environment can also foster conversations with an employee about not being a good fit in their current position. There may be an opportunity for them to find their passion elsewhere within the company or in an entirely different company. In the end, there is more success and satisfaction for all involved.

There they are, a few skills of visionary leaders creating an employee experience people want. Can you improve on being a great listener, open to new ideas, consistently growing and creating a safe environment? If you had all four of these attributes being demonstrated in your company, you could have the same kind of success as these companies in this book have had. But they don't rest on their laurels. The reason these attributes work is because these organizations have built them into the fabric of their everyday life within their organization.

These companies understand that employee engagement is just a piece of what is now the employee experience. At one point in time, we all thought it was important to have wellness programs. Now, we realize what we're really striving for is well-being. That's what happened with employee engagement. We realized that employee engagement is a segment of the overall employee experience.

The employee experience starts when someone sees a job that you're offering. How is it written? What's in it for them? What do they see that would make them say, "I want to work there." It continues into what happens in someone's daily life within your company. It starts with an onboarding process and continues on a daily basis. How are they greeted into your organization? What process keeps them apprised of the company's future and how they contribute? Are they given the tools and skills they need to succeed? Further into the employee experience is the existence of exit strategies. Do you have any? In the past, employees were always warned to not burn any bridges when they left. The same goes for the employer as well.

That same person who leaves your company could refer you excellent candidates or customers. Celebrate their success. Why have people walk out the door angry?

Each of these elements are explored in the following chapters. I'm quite sure you will find something within these pages you can utilize in your own organization. Remember, life is not a destination, but a journey. In the same vein, the employee experience should be created to continue as long as your organization is around. What that looks like depends on what you create.

As I read and edit these transcripts for you, it is such a joy to reacquaint myself with the relationships I've built with these visionary leaders. Their true authenticity seeps through everything they do. What you'll find throughout is that these companies are a place where people go to work and want to be there.

As I end my shows, I end this chapter:

Until next time, this is Julie Ann Sullivan saying, thank you for taking the time in your day to be here. You can always visit us at BusinessesThatCarePodcast.com. Remember, simple solutions can create big results. Go out there and make a difference.

Favorite Food: Chocolate

CREATING FUN AS A BUSINESS CULTURE

WITH BILL HAGAMAN, CEO, WITHUMSMITH+BROWN

*"If you don't have ideas that don't work,
then you don't have enough ideas."*

Bill Hagaman

BILL HAGAMAN IS CEO and the managing partner and CEO of WithumSmith+Brown, (WSB), an accounting firm. When somebody suggested that WSB be on Businesses That Care podcast, my first thought was, an accounting firm? Since I am a recovering accountant, I was very intrigued. We don't think of an accounting firm as a place where people have fun. But after watching the videos from this firm, I almost wanted to go back to being an accountant well, almost. On the WSB website, their career page says, "Surround yourself with exceptional talent and exceptional human beings. Put yourself in a position of strength." I love the fact that Bill's organization realizes the importance of human relationships. After doing my research, looking at the WSB website and watching their entertaining videos, I was so delighted that there is a large accounting firm out there that actually cares about their people and knows how to work hard and have fun. It is proof that no matter what industry you are in, business culture matters. Get ready to take some notes because there are a lot of ideas in this chapter.

CONVERSATION WITH JULIE ANN AND BILL:

Julie Ann: When you started out in accounting the very first place you worked . . . was it fun?

Bill: Well, I've been at Withum since 1980, and it was the second place I've worked. And I have to say that it has always been fun. The founders here made sure they created an atmosphere that was relaxed and put our people first. I've always enjoyed that, and I've worked hard to carry that legacy on.

Julie Ann: That's almost revolutionary.

Bill: I remember Ivan Brown in 1980 or 1981, looking at a survey and saying that companies change accounting firms not because of fees, but because of service and because of the people they are dealing with. That was right up there as one or two. He made a concerted effort to put our people up front and it has worked. It is something we want to continue to do as we move forward into the future.

Julie Ann: Would you speak a little bit about one or two ideas that you utilize in putting people first, and therefore, creating more productivity, better problems-solvers, and better customer services?

Bill: There are many things we do in order to engage our team members. One is that we call them team members. We try to stay away from other types of vernacular like staff or employees. Some of our new ideas include complete flex scheduling. We book work for anytime they want, when they want. We have "dress for your day," which seems kind of silly, but when you walk around and talk to millennials, it's important to them. They want to wear jeans if they aren't going to see a client that day, or they know the client doesn't care. We have a number of team member engagement committees. We have just set up what we call, "team member advisory boards," which are done by level. Team members are elected from each office. They are going to meet with our talent development department each month to talk about how we can make our firm better. We have also recently set up an innovation council. We have put together nine people across our geographic spectrum, across our service spectrum, and across our various experience levels. Their job is to think about the future. How to make the firm better and how we can innovate. We are looking for ways to innovate better service: how we can innovate our services with the clients; how we can innovate to deliver services; and how we can innovate our back office. That is a group that will meet eight to ten times a year. I've got a wonderful person running that who used to do this for the large Big Four firms. But the point is that all of these types of programs promote engagement by our team members. I want them to think about how important it is and how much fun it is to work here, how flexible we are, and how we are putting them ahead of everything else. We start with our team members, and great team members bring in great clients. Great clients then attract even better team members, and we just continue to move that way.

Julie Ann: It is interesting when you were talking about that because sometimes I think the most obvious ideas are the ones that certain organizations totally miss. You value having your own team members come up with new concepts. Unfortunately a lot of organizations don't. So many times, either talent directors or HR directors, come in and decide what is going to be best for the people who are representing the organization and doing a lot of the work, instead of asking them, "Hey, can we work together to come up with the best solution for what ultimately you are going to be involved with?" It seems so obvious, yet there are so many people who are not including the work force in deciding what is best for them. I was thinking about what you said about dress for the day. Really, why get all dressed up if you are just going to be sitting at a desk working on a project all day. I want to be as comfortable as possible. A focus of this podcast is about Simple Solutions for Big Results. Something simple, like how one dresses, can make a big difference on how well someone works throughout their day. Also, if they feel like they are getting dressed up and that is a waste of time and energy, they aren't working their best because they have those thoughts going through their head, right? Our brain only has so much room, so if in their head, they are thinking about how ridiculous it is that they need to wear a suit that day, then they don't have all their brain power and focus on the work at hand. Quality will obviously go up when including these people in their own engagement, just by asking them to be part of the process.

Bill: It is amazing. One of the other things we do that I didn't mention is, we have a suggestion box. We generally get 15 to 20 suggestions on a monthly basis. Our executive or management committee will look at those. Then, I send an email out to the entire firm: Here is the suggestion, and here is why we did it or here is why we didn't do it. The thought being that when we don't do something, we are able to explain the business rationale. It's amazing because sometimes we get suggestions we just wouldn't think of and they are great suggestions. Because they are coming from the ground level, from the people who are doing the work every day, and those of us on the master committee, who haven't prepared a tax return or done an audit, or a financial statement . . .

Julie Ann: Or have used a new procedure, new software, or whatever.

Bill: Correct. So, it makes it much easier. We get great, great ideas out of our suggestions box.

Julie Ann: And you show respect for the people who are doing the work that you are not doing, by recognizing their willingness to come forward. By acknowledging their ideas. I love the idea of being able to say to people, we listened to your idea and this is why we didn't choose it, instead of ignoring the suggestion. You get buy-in because they understand that you listened to the idea.

Bill: Absolutely right.

Julie Ann: Let's talk a bit about your videos. (Find a link at the end of this chapter) They are so much fun! I found myself getting up and dancing. So if the listeners are wondering how that is possible, you have to watch them. They are annual, right?

Bill: Yes. Basically, the story behind the videos is in conjunction with another program to employ team member engagement. We bring all of our 900-team members together once a year. And they come from all our different geographies; we're flying people in from Boston, Florida, etc. What happens is at these meetings we look for something to kick off the meeting that was going to be light and funny. One of my partners came up with let's do a video. He had seen a lip-synched video done by the people on the Today Show. And this was six or seven years ago. We figured we would try it. And we wanted it for that one purpose. Turns out with all the social media opportunities, our team members loved it so much they were broadcasting it all over the place. So we weren't able to keep it quiet, and it has become an annual program for us. We have a lot of fun doing the filming, it has become a culture event for us. Everybody enjoys the filming, and it really brings all of our people together. We spend about a week filming and then we have a big wrap party. We put a call-out every year for volunteers and not by surprise, the 150-200 people who volunteer happen to be our superstars. It's a better way to engage them in the firm. The side benefit is with the video being a peek into our culture and the marketers loved it. It has helped us in recruiting people and bringing in new business. It's really become the thing we are known for, and it helps us differentiate ourselves in a marketplace where there is a lot of "sameness." It was something we did on a lark. It was something we didn't expect this kind of long-term benefit from, but we are very happy with and pleased with its success.

Julie Ann: I would imagine, too, that the people who volunteer to be in it almost become "invisible mentors" for other people who might look at them and say, I didn't really want to do that, but look, they did it and it was so much fun. Maybe I'll push myself a little out of my comfort zone next year. Have you found that at all?

Bill: Absolutely. That first year we put the call out, we got about 30 people. I was going around "twisting arms" trying to get people to participate. Then, everybody saw how much fun it was. Now, we are trying to find roles for everybody because we don't want to exclude anybody

	who volunteers. Even when I am recruiting senior people, they ask me how they can get into next year's video. So it's actually very cool.
Julie Ann:	Something to strive for, right? Some people want to be a partner, and some people want to be in the video.
Bill:	Exactly. They want to be front and center.
Julie Ann:	That's great! Please talk to us a little bit about your "Ten Elements. (See them at the end of the chapter.) I think that concept, above and beyond what is included in them, is really important to your workplace culture.
Bill:	Sure, Julie Ann. I was concerned about our abilities as we grew. Our growth comes from both acquisitions of accounting consultant firms, as well as organic growth. I was concerned that with all the growth we were going to lose our culture, which we hold near, and dear. We came up with these "Ten Elements" of how we expect people to conduct themselves, and they are qualities we think are important to our culture, and we call them the Withum Way. And I'm not going to go through all ten, but it starts with "Think Client Centrically," so that we are always thinking every day about how we can better serve our clients. It talks about our integrity is not for sale, and how there is nothing more important than our integrity, and we can never compromise that.
Bill:	It talks about living life passionately and how important it is outside of your work life to be passionate about something, whether it is skiing with your children, or the local food bank. It talks about giving back to the community, which is another one of our Elements and how important that is to us. We have been doing that since 1980 and repeat them on a regular basis. When we

have our annual meeting, I make sure I go through all ten. When we go through orientation, I go through all ten. I send out a weekly managing- partner email we call the MP Message. Generally, once I month I do a deep dive into one of the Elements. It is something that we try to make part of our culture and institutionalize our culture so to speak. It has really worked. At first, I thought it was maybe a little corny. But I do have people coming up to me saying that they are living the Withum Way, and the team members really, really enjoy it.

Julie Ann: he beautiful thing about that, of course, is not only does it change their lives within Withum, it changes their lives outside of Withum. And I like that you used the word "institutionalize." I always talk about the need to create ideas that become the fabric of your business. I think it is so important for businesses to understand the importance of repetition. You understand how important that is. You were just talking about the fact that you mention the Elements at the annual meeting, you talk about it when you are doing orientation, and it is constantly around. I'm sure it is around your office, and it's available for people to see all the time. That is so important when you want to change a culture. You aren't going to change a culture overnight; that just doesn't happen. It is a long-term project. My favorite poster was always, "life is a journey, not a destination." I think changing workplace culture is the same way. You don't ever get to a point where you say okay, that's it we are perfect.

Bill: You are never there. I like to say it is a living, breathing thing and we can mess it up at any time. One of the hardest things for me when I took this job over six years ago was getting used to repeating myself. You have to constantly deliver the same message over and over and over again. That's the only way it works. You get your talking points, get your messaging you want to do, make sure you use the right language because words are very important, and you've got to constantly say it. You've got to constantly drive it home. Many times I tell my partners that one of my biggest roles is to be the firm's head cheerleader. That is one of the jobs on top of vision and everything else; vision and strategy and making sure you are getting the messaging right.

Julie Ann: And you have to do it in a creative way because if you keep doing it the same old way all the time, its emphasis gets dissipated. You are always finding new ways. Is there anything you guys did that didn't work? Can you talk about something you thought was going to be a great idea, but it didn't work out?

Bill: There have been ideas that didn't work. We tried to come up with a diary, so to speak. I believe in the Zappos book by Tony Hsieh, they have a diary or some type of catalogue they keep, where people write good things about the organization. So we tried that, and everybody on our marketing team wrote something and nobody else did. So that is something that kind of fell flat. There have been one or two other things. You try, and we like to use the term around here "fail-pass." It's okay to have ideas that don't work, but you just got to move on from them. If you don't have ideas that don't work, then you don't have enough ideas. So we just continue to roll things out, if they don't work and fall flat, then you move forward. You hope you don't spend a ton of money on the stuff that doesn't work. When they do work, you continue to try to make them better year after year. Something like our annual meeting really works, and it's gotten to be very expensive, but it works. And we continue every year to do better than we did the year before.

Julie Ann: And that's a great challenge to have, right? How can we do this better?

Bill: I drive my partners and all of our admin staff here nuts because I'm always telling them we have to be better than last year. We are a great firm, and if we are going to continue to be a great firm, we have to be better than we were last year. We need to move the dial. So, nobody can rest on their laurels, nobody can say we've been doing it this way forever. We need to rethink it, and we need to continue to move forward. That's very, very important to me and it has become part of our culture at the firm.

Julie Ann: I'm sure that filters down into each individual's work, too, right? If you are looking at your firm with an overall philosophy of constantly getting better at what you do, then each individual understands they need to continue to improve as well. It's not like it's a mandate the C-Suite is not following, everyone is following it.

Bill: You've got to follow it in order to keep up. It's very important people keep up with us. We try to have the best; everybody says that, we try to practice it. It is important to us that you strive to be the best, in order to continue to work for us and be part of our team. We are constantly looking at that.

Julie Ann: One of the things I talked to you about was utilizing this podcast that we're doing as a recruitment tool. Some of the companies I've been working with have been playing it for people they are recruiting. They have them listen to it as part of the interview process because it is a part of the culture. You and I both know that recruiting is a key beginning. If you recruit well, everything else goes a lot smoother than if you don't recruit smart. Do you have them watch your videos or do you wonder if they watched the videos, before they come in for that interview?

Bill: I think it has been pretty standard these days that candidates look at the website. So I'd be shocked if they have not looked at our videos coming in. When we are out doing recruiting at schools, we certainly use the videos as one of our talking points. Therefore, it is something we bring front and center during our process.

Julie Ann: You're showing them what your culture is like. When job seekers look at the video, they might say that's too much for me. And that's fine. It saves everyone a lot of time and energy.

Bill: I tell people all the time that we are not for everybody, and that's okay, we can still be friends. We are trying to get the best and the brightest in order to service our clients, in order for us to continue to get better clients. Our expectations are high (when people start), and we don't make excuses for it. You've got to be good to work here.

Julie Ann: I'm sure you are constantly growing because you have this idea of institutionalizing ideas. You not only move them forward, you live them. If you had to pick one that you think is just the essence of who Withum is, what would that be?

Bill: It's probably our annual meeting. Here are a couple things we do at that annual meeting. I speak about where the firm has been the past year. I speak a little about where we expect the firm is going. I talk a little about the macroeconomic impacts that we may be looking to impact us over the next 12 months. But more importantly, I put up on the board, a full projection of where we expect the firm to grow in terms of revenue, in terms of the number of people, and in terms of the number of partners. We project how many partners we need to add to support our growth, our organic growth and to be able to retire-out our partners that are reaching the normal retirement age. We also give out awards, which we call "Strength Awards;" our tag line is, "Be in a Position of Strength." So we have awards called, "Strength in Client Service," "Strength in Community," "Strength in Innovation." And we treat it almost like a bit of the Academy Awards. We do a video, and there are generally five, six, or seven nominees in each category. We do a short video of each one. Then, we have the winner from the prior year stand up and open an envelope and say, "The winner is . . . "

Julie Ann: Do you have a red carpet?

Bill: We don't do the red carpet, but they walk up in front of their 900 teammates and receive their award. The important thing for me is as we are showing the videos of what the nominees did, hopefully we have 900 people sitting there thinking: I want to be up there next year. What can I do to make the firm better, what can I do to innovate, to do a great job at client service so that I get recognition? I think that's very important. We are showing the qualities that we hold in importance and our team members all are able to see that. That's probably the one thing we do the best and has really worked the best over the years.

Creating Fun As A Business Culture

Julie Ann: Thanks, Bill. I really had a great time with you on Businesses That Care. I find you to be extremely intelligent and kind, just a class act. I am really glad you are out there for the people in your firm and all the people they touch in the world around you. Thanks very much for being with us.

Bill: Thank you, Julie Ann. Have a great day.

Favorite Food: Peanut Butter

WithumSmith+Brown are big thinkers and have lofty goals. It is not a place to work and be complacent. They are very up front about that, which is why they achieve such excellence in people and services. Bill has instilled an atmosphere where team members know they have a voice. They know they are a part of a community that not only is open to new ideas, but also is willing to try them, or at least tell them why not.

You may not come away from this chapter wanting to produce a music video, but there are plenty of ways to increase the engagement and support of your team members. WSB includes their team members in creating many of the changes within the company. By setting up councils with a plan, team members immediately understand that their input is being valued...before they ever begin. That is a tremendous way to grow creativity.

The best accounting firm I ever worked in was one where I had the most fun. Consequently, I also worked my best. The two can coincide. Don't underestimate the value of fun.

WithumSmith+Brown Culture Video 2018 - bit.ly/WSBCultureVideo2018

THE TEN ELEMENTS OF THE WITHUM WAY

1. Think Client Centrically
2. Possess a Vision for Growth
3. Welcome Innovation and Change
4. Maintain a Cooperative Attitude
5. Demand Integrity
6. Cultivate Open and Honest Relationships
7. Embrace the Family Spirit
8. Work hard/Play hard
9. Give Back
10. Live Life Passionately

WHEN YOUR WITCHCRAFT IS YOUR BEST STRENGTH

WITH TANA GREENE, CEO, THE GREENE GROUP

"Say It, Mean It, Do It"
Tana Greene

TODAY I HAVE THE 'QUEEN OF THE ROAD' with me. If you don't know what I'm referencing there's a great article in *INC* magazine, and that's what it was called, "Queen of the Road." As I read through this article, I discovered the diverse and amazing life Tana has lived. She's had her share of hardship, but her own style of "Witchcraft" has made her very successful, personally and professionally. This witchcraft is based on 4 core values.

1. **Never Settle**.

   (I'm all about that.)

2. **If you say it, you better mean it, and you better do it**.

   (Being an accountability freak, I love that one!)

3. **Dare to be different.**

   (How do we grow if we are not willing to do something different?)

4. **See the awesomeness in others.**

   (Search for the awesomeness in others in places you might not think of looking.)

I was so impressed with what Tana has done for her workplace culture, that I reached out to her immediately after reading the article. I did and she granted me time to come on and share her style of witchcraft with you.

CONVERSATION WITH JULIE ANN AND TANA:

Julie Ann: Hey there, Tana! Thanks so much for taking time out of your busy day to spend with us.

Tana: Thank you, Julie Ann. I'm glad you found the article, and I'm glad you have me on the show. Hopefully, we'll be able to spread this "Witchcraft."

Julie Ann: Why don't you tell our audience just a little bit about your background, and what made you care about workplace culture?

Tana: Actually, as you said, I went through some hardship, and I came out on the other side. When you get to a certain point, you decide, well. . .what do I want to be?

I knew I wanted to own my own business; at 17 I wrote it as a goal on a piece of paper. So, at 29, I opened the doors of my business in 1988. It was to help people get jobs. That's what I wanted to do, make a difference in people's lives, and get them jobs. So my husband and I began the business together, 50-50 right out of the gate. We started doing clerical placements. We created a niche within manufacturing distribution, where we would place large-volume, temporary workers that would eventually go on permanent with the company as they had openings. That spread nationally.

Then, we said, well, we manufacture the product, we help package the product, but somebody has to drive the product. So we said let's open a company. In 2009, we opened Road Dog Drivers, a truck staffing and recruiting service. That was to provide the professional truck driver. In the last three years, there had been a shortage of drivers, and extreme inefficiency in the marketplace. I created a marketplace, for the gig economy, for professional truck drivers. They didn't have anywhere to go to find a just-in-time job when they needed it. Or, they wanted to supplement: "I'm not getting enough hours," or the "I want to be my own boss," or "I want to drive when I want, where I want, for whom I want." Unless you had your own truck, you couldn't do that. So, Blue Bloodhound was created in 2015, to match truck drivers with motor carriers. To me, there's no shortage of drivers; there is an inefficiency of matching the driver that is ready to drive with the qualifications. So, that's my latest venture, and it's going really well so far.

One of the things I would like to share is that I didn't understand the importance of culture and value, until about 10 years ago. I had allowed the traditional business model to drive everything. I started out helping people, then it became about the money. As we grew and got thousands of employees, and things were starting to spread, I realized I was losing something.

I found myself not joyful anymore. I thought to myself, I really have to get out of this business because I have to go do my calling. I'm not joyful. I'm not happy. So, obviously, I have to leave this to go do something else. I hired a coach.

I hired a coach, and the coach said to me, "Why can't you do your calling in your business?" And I said, "Because it's not there." The coach said, "If you really understood who you were, and what your values are, and you worked it from there, then your business would change." And I thought, "How do you do that?"

First, I went on the journey of understanding who I was.

I started with StrengthsFinder, and I really looked at those profiles to find out what am I. Then, I started to say, what are my values, and what does that even mean? How do you build that into a culture? With a lot of work, and a lot of writing, I really identified first of all, what am I really good at doing? Second of all, what are the things that are important to me?

Every one of those values you mentioned has a story to me.

When I think about *Never Settle*, I remember what I went through getting married at a very young age. I was 15. My son was born when I was 16. At 17, I realized I was in a violent domestic relationship with a ninth-grade education.

At that time, I said, "I'm not going to' settle." I wrote four goals on a piece of paper when I left him:

1. I'm going to own my own home by the time I'm 25.

2. I was going to marry a knight in shining armor.

3. I was going to finish my education.

4. I was going to own my own business by the time I was 30.

Well, I finished school. I accomplished buying my first home at 22. I married my husband of 32 years now when I was 26 and started my business at 29. What I realized was that setting goals, deciding never to settle, and knowing what you want, was really important in life. These ideas had to be the driving value within business and they came from within me as something really important.

Here's the story behind *Say It, Mean It, Do It*. My father was the ultimate mentor to me. When he passed away, I will never forget the men of the church stood up and said, "He never talked the talk, but he walked the walk." To me that meant, if you say it, you mean it and you're going to do it. That's customer service, that's pleasing people, getting things done for them, and it is another important value in business.

The *Dare To Be Different* came from when I was moved to an all-black school in 1971. It was a middle school, and it was the first time they had ever de-segregated in the town I grew up in, which was in Virginia. We got to school, and the parents were enraged. They said, "My children are not going to another school, not going to happen." They put us on that little yellow bus and we went anyway. The principal decided I was the leader. I began the year with devotions, back when you could do that, over a loudspeaker. And it was daring to be different. He was different to begin with, and then he helped me come through that as well. I learned, just be yourself, let it go, and understand who you are, was really, really important. That is what I want to be able to pull that out of my employees.

The 4th core value is, *See the Awesomeness In Others*. When I was 15, and I went to my mother to tell her I was pregnant, she turned to me and she said, "I'm so happy, I was afraid I was going to be too old to be a grandmother." Now, you know that's not what she was thinking. But, she saw the awesomeness in me, and in the moment.

The way it made me feel was that unconditional love was important to build into everything we do as individuals in our lives.

So, these were the four values that we set. But then, it was how do you spread that amongst an organization that is in 26 states? And last year we had 10,000 W-2s. How do you do that? We started a process of "What did I do?" I started with taking the StrengthsFinder test. Every employee has to take the StrengthsFinder test. They start really looking at the top strengths that they have. Then, we try to marry those into what they are doing every day. What I learned is that when you know how you are making a difference, and what you are doing to make that difference, then you are a much happier, connected employee. People have left because of it, because they found it wasn't right for them. And I would rather them exit at that point, than to get deep into it and be very dissatisfied.

I also wrote a book in 2012: *Creating a World of Difference*. And it really goes into all of our values, and why. It tells all these stories.

We have a council that is broken up into multi-segments of our business, where they meet to talk about each one of these values, and how we are meeting those within the organization.

My husband, my partner, who is just wonderful, and my COO used to say, "There she goes with that 'Witchcraft.'" That was always their big thing when I would come down the hall preaching some value, and they would say, "There she goes with that 'Witchcraft, again.'"

Yet, as our business began to scale and went from 19 million to 29 million to 49 million to 65 million, they all went, "Okay, we get your 'Witchcraft' now."

Julie Ann: There are a couple of things I really love about what you have been saying. I think it is worth going over again because they are so important. First of all, you started with *you*. And I think there are a lot of companies out there that want to know what to do for with their culture, but they don't start with themselves. You have to start with yourself because you don't know what you are teaching someone else or may not know what you are doing. That's number one. Number two, I love the fact that you say it's a lot of work. It is a lot of work and is a continuum of work. I have warned audiences that if somebody is willing to come in and tell you if you just pay them for a two-hour presentation they are going to change your culture, then run as fast as you can. That is not going to happen.

You have councils. I like to create a culture council in companies that don't have it because you are engaging people right away by asking their opinion.

As you mentioned, it is so important to realize that it is okay for people to exit. I think this is so important. Honestly, most of the companies I have had on Businesses That Care, do talk about the fact that sometimes there is not a good fit.

I had a coach who taught me that a person and a job may not be a good fit and that is not personal, right?

Tana: Right.

Julie Ann: My guests have been using these podcasts as a recruiting tool. They have prospects listen to them. Some say,

"Wow, I want to work for that company," while others say, "That's not my style." Isn't it great to find out before you sign the paperwork?

Tana: Yes, sometimes you don't quite know that, but the quicker the exit, the better if it is not a fit.

Julie Ann: I love the idea of everyone doing StrengthsFinder, and finding their strength and matching it to their work. Some people go into a job thinking they want to do it and discover they don't like it. However, if nobody ever talks to them, they may assume they are not a good worker instead of the possibility that they just don't like what they are doing. The StrengthsFinder can really help with that. How do you think this way of thinking has really affected what comes out of your company to your clients and your customers?

Tana: It really comes down to being authentic. When you allow yourself to be humble to a level where you are willing to share your story, and you are willing to share your strengths and your weaknesses with your staff, then it gives them permission to go the other way. So they are not as afraid to say, "I don't know," or "That didn't work for me." We live in this world of The Big Lie I call it. We want everyone to believe we are perfect and that we do everything perfectly, and we don't ever want them to see that side that might not be quite exactly what we want them to see. What I have learned is that when I finally gave that up, and I started being who I was and who I was created to be, all of a sudden my world opened up; it changed. My employees then changed because they became authentic, and they felt they could be who they are. So, I would say it is being pure authentic and teaching people to be that way.

Julie Ann: It is interesting, and I'm sure you read a lot. One of the things I've noticed is there are a lot of articles out now about how good leaders need to be vulnerable. And, allow people who work with them, know they are not a god or goddess. They are a human being. And they make mistakes, and they don't feel good some days, and they don't always feel they perform their best, and in sharing that, they allow people to see, that person is just like me, and I could rise to her level because she is like me and she did it. That makes for better employees.

How do you think your customers feel? Do you think they get this flow of change?

Tana: Absolutely. We share with them our values, we share with them what we want to do when we go into contract with our clients, and we sit down and talk with them about it.

What I try to teach my staff is as you are interacting with your customer, don't be afraid to actually verbalize what you are doing there. We don't want to align ourselves with companies that don't have the same type of values that we do. We have walked away from clients because otherwise what you are doing is subjecting your employees to a very bad situation, basically telling them because of revenues you have to keep doing business with them. So. We flush through that pretty quickly, even in the "dating" scene, before we "marry" them. We try to get through that process because it is never going to work if your values don't match.

Julie Ann:	I agree. You have to be willing to let some business go because in the long run they are just going to drain your energy, and I've found they don't pay their bills!
Tana:	That's true because they don't have good values, right? Right!
Julie Ann:	Right! And that becomes a lesson in how much do you think you are worth? Do you really need to work with somebody who doesn't have your values?
Tana:	Right! You don't. And it really hurts your culture if you do.
Julie Ann:	I have found that the less hungry and more authentic, really makes your company stand out. The customers and clients your getting are going to stand out as well.
Tana:	Absolutely.
Julie Ann:	Now what are you going to do? What are you going to continue to do? What's your next tweak in your business?
Tana:	Most of my employees out of the 10,000, 140 of them, are my permanent that do my placement. I want to spread this down to the level of the temporary workers themselves and I want them to be able to understand what their purpose is, how it makes a difference, and what their strengths are. So I'm kind of trying to figure out how that could work because it is forever moving. We have so many out there. If we have been able to affect the change within the ranks here, how can we take that to the next level? That's my goal over the next five years, to try to figure that out, and try to perfect that.
Julie Ann:	I have read some research on purpose. It says that if you know your purpose, you actually can lengthen your life.
Tana:	Wow! I want that research.

Julie Ann: I'll send it to you.

Other research shows that when people know, their greater purpose in life, beyond the daily processes, it changes their focus, their quality of work, how hard they work and how responsible they feel about their work. In too many companies people knowing their purpose is missing.

Tana: Yes, it is. There is a book called, The *On-Purpose Person*, and *The On-Purpose* Business Person, by Kevin McCarthy. You end up with a two-words for your statement of your purpose at the end of the workbook.

Mine is Igniting Joy. Once I realized it is what I am here to do, everything filters through that before I accept doing anything because it's who I am, and that's what I am here to do. He is actually working on a tool that you may go on an app, do a test, and then come up with your two-word statement. I'm excited to be with him through that process. But it is all about "why am I here." Once you figure that out, your life simplifies. It is the craziest thing. I was at a conference recently and there was a speaker named Shawn Achor who wrote, *The Happiness Advantage*. He made a statement, and I keep telling everybody because it meant so much to me: Happiness is a choice, but joy comes from fulfilling potential. And I just went WOW! Because you can choose to be happy or not happy, but really, if you are doing everything you can to understand what your strengths are and putting them to work—we are given those basic strengths at birth—they don't change, but we choose to either exercise them or we don't. It's the same thing with a muscle, it either builds or it doesn't. I realized that fulfilling that potential of those strengths you have is really where you find your joy and purpose, which falls in with all of that. It does make a huge difference.

Julie Ann: Absolutely. For me, it is positivity. Everything I want to do, I want to do from the eye of positivity. And I admit in ten seconds I could be a puddle on the floor. I've got plenty of stuff I can say is horrible if that's what I choose to bring into my life. That's true for everybody. Everyone has stuff, everyone, whether it is from the past, from their current situation, or their fears of the future. It is a choice. I know they are there; I'm not living in rose-colored glasses. I choose to look at what is the positivity and how can I share that. I talked to a friend today. I'm going to be in their neck of the woods, so I asked if I could stop by. One of the things my friend said to me before she got off the phone was, "You made my day." I paused for a minute, and said, "That's a really nice thing to say." Instead of ignoring it, I recognized that is really special that I made someone's day. Those are the kinds of choices we make. When we are in business, it is so easy to not notice.

Tana: You get caught up in the day-to-day, trying to drive revenues, trying to control cost, and you forget those things, the human part of it. In my book, *Creating a World of Difference*, I talk about creating a world of difference. I say you don't wait until you have $100,000 to donate. My husband is the best at this, he can be at McDonald's and he will use that employee's name, and he will ask them how they are. That little connection created a world of difference. Just like it did with your friend when you said you were going to stop by to see them, which was going to make their day. And I think if we concentrate on being positive, making a difference in someone's life, then our whole world will change if we could all do that.

Julie Ann: I am with you on that. On my Facebook page it says, I just want to change the world, one person at a time. There it is. It is as simple as that. And you have done that for me today.

Tana: Good! I'm glad! I did ignite joy then!

Julie Ann: What you don't know is that I have a dog named Joy.

Tana: WOW!

Julie Ann: And I named her Joy purposely because I can walk with Joy, and sleep with Joy, and come home to Joy, and play with Joy!

Tana: That's great.

Julie Ann: It is very strategic. I purposely picked that name so I would have Joy in my life every day.

Tana: That is really cool. What kind of dog is it I have to ask?

Julie Ann: She is an apricot poodle. I will send you a picture. She is adorable, and a really good girl. It's funny because people will say, oh, you have Joy in your life. And I say, "I know. I did it on purpose." I think there are a lot of things we can do in our lives and in our business lives to bring this in, you know. I was recently a guest on a podcast and we talked about positivity. I said, I must have a hundred items in my little tiny house, and about fifty of them are in my office to remind me of the person I want to be.

Tana: That's a good reminder. Visuals are so important for that. Writing the goals and having visuals to attach to are critical for this journey.

Julie Ann: You and I are like twins.

Tana: Yes, I think so!

Julie Ann: There's a listener out there and they haven't even thought about engagement or workplace culture yet. Believe me, there are plenty of people out there just realizing that this is something they have to work on. What would you tell them Step One is?

Tana: Step One is work on yourself. Hire a coach. Find someone who can help you grow. Go take the StrengthsFinder test, and don't just look at it and put it down, look at it once a week, twice a week, study it, and start marrying what you are enjoying doing with your strengths. Do more of those, and then, help your employees do that as well.

Julie Ann: That is great. Thank you so much for being with us today.

Tana: Thank you, Julie Ann.

Favorite Food: French Fries

Here is a woman whose life was not filled with the easiest or most supportive of circumstances. She didn't settle. With her lofty written goals and a huge dose of determination, she has become very successful in her personal and professional life. Finding her purpose and strengths, she can now pass those skills onto her employees. What was validated for me by Tana Greene is the importance of authenticity and self-exploration. You cannot have one without the other.

A great leader is real. Employees today are smarter than ever and their BS meters are very sensitive. They want to work with C-Suite executives they can relate to. The only way to feel comfortable with yourself, enough to be authentic, is with the dedication and acceptance that self-exploration is a continuous growth process. Show your workforce you have that ability and they will grow with you and look forward to it.

CODE OF VALUES

WITH MARY THOMPSON, COO, DWYER GROUP[1]

"It is a lot easier to hold people accountable when you first ask them to hold you accountable."

Mary Thompson

MARY THOMPSON IS THE CHIEF OPERATING OFFICER of the Dwyer Group. The Dwyer Group has many well-known service companies under its umbrella such as, Mr. Rooter, Mr. Handyman and Molly Maids. My desire to talk with Mary came from the understanding that the Dwyer Group was keen on the importance of repetition and reinforcement. An idea I believe is missing in the desire for persistent and consistent change. In this interview Mary shares the company's values and the importance of having them. It sounds so obvious, but at the Dwyer Group they have unique ways of internalizing those values. For instance, at company meetings, employees are encouraged to recite the company's code of values, with heart. The employee receives a certificate and $50 gift card. Why? Because the Dwyer Group understands the necessity of repetition and reinforcement, to allow these values to become a part of the fabric of their company. The main principles of their code of values are the idea of living "R.I.C.H." with respect, integrity, customer focus and having fun.

---

1 Dwyer Group formally changed its name to Neighborly in September 201

Mary Thompson started her career in the armed services. From rappelling out of helicopters and managing an airfield in Korea, to working in recruitment for the Marine Corps. Thompson says, "It wasn't about going down the easy road, it was about being the best person you can be and that's about doing the right thing. I've found that doing the right thing is rarely about doing the easiest things. I didn't take the comfortable path, I always believed a comfortable path is the most dangerous path you can take." Not only that, but she is a licensed plumber, like she says, she was a woman living in the old boys' club in many different arenas. I just love that.

CONVERSATION WITH JULIE ANN AND MARY

Julie Ann: The company she works for has had 100-percent growth in the last two years. Is that right?

Mary: It sure is!

Julie Ann: That is crazy and still people like working for you all. No small achievement. One of the things we are going to talk about today is their Code of Values. One of the reasons I really respect this organization is that too many companies have great mission statements and values statements, but they don't carry it through their company, but you do. Why don't you tell us about that Mary, and your background?

Mary: Thank you, Julie Ann. Thank you for inviting me to have this conversation with you. We love talking about our Code of Values and who we are. I always tell everybody, don't tell me your beliefs–show me. I really don't care about your beliefs; your behavior will tell me exactly who you are. And what I love about our Code of Values is that it is a set of rules we can live by. You bring a bunch of people together that belong. I read a really good book not long ago called, *The Gifts of Imperfection* and it talks about fitting in and belonging.

Julie Ann: Brené Brown?

Mary: Yes. It's a great read. We are belongers. What happens when you have this set of rules on the way you want to do things, other people who belong, who ascribe to those same set of values, start coming on board with you. A lot of our magic comes from our values we call living RICH. That stands for Respect, Integrity, Customer focus, and my favorite one, Having fun in the process.

Julie Ann: I knew I liked you for a good reason.

Mary: I actually think one of our most important values is having fun in the process, because you think about how many hours a day you spend away from your family and important people in your lives so you can earn a living. If you are not having fun, if you don't bring fun to the associates in your team, then they don't bring fun to the client or customer, and then the customer is not happy. You don't wake up in the morning thinking, yay I'm going to spend $3,000 to replace my sewer line. We are definitely a "grudge" purchase in a lot of our brand. So having fun is about taking that moment and bringing a little joy into what's happening because that moment is going to happen whether you are having fun or not.

Julie Ann: Let's take a step back, can you give our listeners a little overview of what the Dwyer Group is?

Mary: Certainly. We are in the service business. We repair, maintain and enhance space. Most anything you would have done in your home or commercial property, we probably do. Anything from our largest brand, Mr. Rooter, I love that brand, in plumbing to heating, and air conditioning with Air Serve. If you need your home painted, we have 5-Star Pro-tech Painters. If you want your home or commercial grounds maintained, we have The Grounds Guys. If you want the inside of your house kept orderly and clean, we have Molly Maids. If you have a refrigerator that needs repair, we have Mr. Appliance. If you want to install a fan in your house, we have Mr. Electric. If you have odds and ends repairs, we have Mr. Handyman. If you have a natural disaster (and you need your home restored, we have a restoration company called Rainbow. Need your windows cleaned? We have Window Genie. About a month ago, I had my windows cleaned by Window Genie, and I was shocked at how bright they looked because I hadn't had my windows cleaned in 10 or 11 years. I was so surprised at how much it really brightened the home up.

Julie Ann: If there were a downside to that Mary, it would be, once you do it you are going to notice the difference and do it again.

Mary: It was really kind of embarrassing to know I had let my windows get that dirty.

Julie Ann: You have to keep getting them done now.

Mary: Yes, yes. So, we do all things in the home. If you think of all things to keep your home in good working order, we do that. Probably what brings me the most joy and satisfaction in my professional life is our mission statement, which is, to teach our principles and systems of personal and business success so that all people we touch live happier and more successful lives. By all people, we mean our franchisees, employees of our franchisees, we mean our customer, we mean our vendor partners, and anybody we touch. That could mean talking to a group of people that listened to this podcast, or standing on a stage talking to franchisers, or working alongside franchisees helping them take their business to a whole new level, all making for a happier and more successful life.

Julie Ann: Yeah, the whole idea of leaving your personal life at home is a joke. It's companies like yours that realize that, and so you are servicing the whole person and not just what you want out of them at work.

Mary: We are. We actually call it the Wheel of Life. Dina Dwyer-Owens, who is co-chair of our board, and has been part of the Dwyer fabric since the very early days, she does a class called Design Your Life. In that class we talk about the Wheel of Life. There are six spokes on this wheel: one spoke is Knowledge, one spoke is Spirituality, one spoke is Financial, one spoke is Health and the other two are Social and Family. If you have a spoke that is not right, your wheel is not right, and you kind of walk through life on an uneven roll. They really all go hand in hand.

Julie Ann: Let's talk a little bit about your Code of Values because I know it is very important for you not only to have them, but to have them seep into the people that you work with. That's what makes your culture stand out. I also want you to talk about how it evolved. I am sure it wasn't in one short meeting.

Mary: No, it did not. When our founder, Don Dwyer Sr., passed away in 1994, the leadership of the company was very concerned that we would lose our values. He had a set of values that he talked about, but when you lose a founder, often the company will lose their way. The leadership group got together and they operationalized the values. We have 15 values under Live R.I.C.H. For instance, under the Respect, the first one is treating others, as you would like to be treated. The next one is listening with the intent to understand what is being said, and acknowledging what is being said is important to the speaker, and I could go on and on. I always have to laugh when we talk about listening with the intent to understand because I often listen with the intent to reply and have to remember to focus on listening with the intent to understand.

Julie Ann: That is right. I am a Communications Specialist, and that is extremely common. That's probably the one aspect of listening that most people have to work on. It is not thinking about what you want to say. No worries though, that means you are a Mere Mortal like the rest of us.

Mary: I may have to work at it, but I love it because I have these rules and guidelines that I follow. What they did is they put all 15 values together, and they went out to the entire company and said, here's the deal; these are the values that we think are important and what we are going to focus on. We're not going to ask you to do anything on these values. We ask you to watch us. Watch us and see how we do, and we're going to ask you to hold us accountable. Accountability is a big part of our culture. I think it is a lot easier to hold people accountable when you first ask them to hold you accountable.

Mary: So we developed a thing called the Beep-beep Game. We said to them if you catch us breaking a value, you can beep us. And I get beeped about once a month. Usually, one of our values under Respect is speaking calmly and respectfully without profanity and without sarcasm.

Every now and then, someone will say Beep to me as I am breaking that value and have to be reminded. We are not a perfect company, and we know we make mistakes every day. But, we get up the next day and we start over. Right now, one of the values I'm really focusing on is "Responding in a Timely Fashion." I've been very busy, and I'm falling behind, and so I've told everybody that I'm working on this, and told them if I am falling behind, let me know. Once everyone saw the leadership really meant it because you can say you have a set of values, but if you are not living them, it doesn't matter. Again, don't tell me what you believe; it's your behavior that makes you a better person, not your beliefs.

Then, we started socializing it out to everybody in the system. And when we have three or more associates that gather, we recite our values. We can do it one of many different ways. Sometimes, we will recite all 15 and then go around the room, and it takes about 47 seconds. Sometimes we recite the Code of Values Statement: Showing respect to all people, acting with integrity, serving customers with focus and enthusiasm, and having fun in the process. So sometimes we start a meeting with that or we will pick one. A couple of days ago we had a meeting, it was a thorny meeting, and there were going to be a lot of tough subjects. Since one of our values is communicating honestly and with purpose, I suggested we start the meeting talking about that. What does that mean? What is purposeful communication? It's not beating around the bush. It means paying attention to what we really need to talk about and being honest about it. In this meeting, I'm asking everybody to communicate honestly and with purpose. Can I get agreement from everyone? Yes.

So each meeting we have, we do it in some way like that. When our franchisees gather, we do the same thing.. They will often recite all 15 values at their team meetings they have once a week.

Julie Ann: I'll ask if you can just travel around in my pocket. I talk to my clients so much about how repetition and reinforcement is king, or queen, as the case may be. It is essential if you want anything to sink in. You can't assume people will remember. And even if they do remember, that reinforcement of actually reciting or talking about what's important is the only way it seeps into the essence of humans and your business. Even when people come on board, and you give them a policy manual, and you say, "Here, read this." And of course, everybody signs off on it, but they never really read it. If you have policies in there that are really important, why don't you talk about them. Have a lunch and learn and go over a really important policy just to make sure that people understand it. Maybe somebody has fine-tuned it or found a better way to do the process or whatever. You've got to keep reinforcing. Your workforce is busy, they can't have every aspect of your business top of mind all the time. They need to be reminded because they are human. We have millions of bits of information coming into our lives every day. So kudos to you for understanding that.

Mary: It is amazing what it does. There are instances where five times a day I'm reciting the values, or I'm listening to a group, who are talking about it, and it starts seeping through and it's woven through all that we do. My favorite way to do it is when we have a larger group; I'll say, "Okay, share to the person on your right which value you think they best represent." It is a great way to compliment one another and also remind people that you are really good. I had someone sitting next to me and I said to them, you operate in a responsible manner, and let me tell you about a time you did that.

Doing something like that makes it very personal to them. We had somebody new here who always recommended picking your favorite one and just owning it. Own it for a month, and tell everybody, this is my favorite one. I'm going to tell you every meeting about my favorite one, and tell them to talk about it. Own it. Mine is Operating in a Responsible Manner: "Above the Line…" I say it so many times I say it too fast now.

Julie Ann: What does that mean?

Mary: It's not just what the contract says to do, it is the spirit and intent of doing the right thing and always the right thing. What did we mean to do? What does the agreement or the conversation mean? That's what operating in a responsible manner is. When we say, "Above the line," we will actually put our hands across horizontally for above the line, and we visually remind people about that. It makes a difference. When we have a company-wide meeting, if someone can recite the Code of Values by heart, with heart, we give him or her $50. I think we have about 60 percent who can recite by heart, with heart. And they get a Live R.I.C.H. shirt, they get the money, and we do it to encourage that and to get people talking about it. I've had conversations starting, "One of our Code of Values is 'responding in a timely fashion,'

Mary, and lately I don't think you have been doing that."
It's a great way to have that reminder.

Julie Ann: I may memorize them just to get the shirt.

Mary: It's a very cool shirt, actually. I love wearing that shirt.

Julie Ann: So, like I said, this idea didn't come out of thin air. You purposely got together and came up with this Code of Values, and you've told us about how you incorporate them within your company. What do you think some of the outcomes have been because of what you do?

Mary: The outcome that fascinates me the most, the first outcome, is that we are a group of belongers, not just within our headquarters, but with our franchisees and their associates as well.

We just did a big survey of the employees of our franchisees, and we asked them; what is the number one reason why you like working here? Number One reason was atmosphere and Code of Values. Number One! This is what happens. The first thing is we attract people who have a like mind to that, which is very good. The second thing that was kind of interesting is that it makes you want to be a better person. We have video of our Chief Information Officer's (CIO) son reciting one of the values in the car on his way to school. The CIO said he realized that these are values that work for his children too. So it starts to weave through the families as well. Then, I also like that it is a set of rules; if I am struggling with something, I can go back to them. It's easier to make a decision when you have a clear set of rules to follow. Lastly, we are in the franchising industry, and I am in the world of service, and sometimes people get a little rough around the edges, they get frustrated. You get very passionate when you are talking about your business, and what your business is. These values help take that passion and hone it to this way of communicating and interacting with one another that makes things happen. I think it's part of, no, I *know* it is part of our growth, it's why we are growing, and it's why we are a profitable company. We have people who have been here for forty years because they want to *belong* to something bigger than themselves. And this helps them do that. I love the stories we give Live R.I.C.H. Awards every quarter. It's stories like, a lady sent a letter in to our CEO, and it said...I was having a bad day, I had a flat tire, and everything was awful. This guy walks up and tells me he is not only going to fix it, but said I'm going to take you to the tire place, and I am going to buy your tire. You just look like a lady who is having a bad day. It was one of our employees. She said, "He was special, and I knew he belonged to something special." So, we give Live R.I.C.H. Awards to celebrate those people who are living those values.

Julie Ann: Great examples! And do you ever utilize your franchisees or their teams to give you feedback to you on how to change the company in better ways? Do you have any incentive programs like that within your Code of Values?

Mary: We survey quite a bit. We survey and ask how are you doing? What should be different? Every one of our brands has an Advisory Council. It is a group of franchisees who are elected, and they meet regularly with the President and leadership of that brand to talk about things. What I love about franchisees is it is a very collaborative process when it is done right and done well. There is a front line. And I think it was Colin Powell who said, "Until proven otherwise, the front line is always right, and the rear echelon isn't. And it is good to remember and stay close to the front line." We have a very formalized process with our advisory councils. A number of times a year we meet with them and we talk through what is working, what might not be working. We talk about how we might want to roll something out, and get their help on what's the best way to roll it out, and listen to all of that. Let's go back to the values for a minute. One of our values is to continuously strive to maximize internal and external customer loyalty. At those advisory meetings, they might say they think we are missing something on internal customer loyalty and here's why we think this. Because we see them as internal customers and the values give us a common language, we can do something about it.

Julie Ann: I think too that with the way you have everything set up, it allows people to become better problem-solvers because you are giving them a voice. Where in companies where people don't really have a voice, they have no avenue to speak up, they have no avenue to make suggestions, or they are concerned about making suggestions, which is horrible. Instead, you are creating people who can have more of a voice because they have a "safe place" to have that voice. Then, they become better problem-solvers on their own.

Mary: You know it's interesting, Matthew Kelly wrote a book called, *Dream Manager*, and in that book, he has a statement that made me think about engagement a lot. And he said for someone to be engaged, they have to believe two things: They have to believe that tomorrow can be bigger than today and they get to be part of it. And so when you have that collaborative process, when you have a common language, when you all belong together, you can start showing that we can make tomorrow better by this, this, and this. Our mission statement includes: To teach our principles and systems of personal and business success so that all people we touch live happier and more successful lives. And, you get to be part of it. Together, we can make that future happen.

Julie Ann: Are there, for lack of a better word, conglomerates that have many franchisees under them like the Dwyer Group? Is it common?

Mary: It's becoming more common. We were doing it long before most were. We've been doing it for more than 30 years now. There has been a move toward like-type franchising businesses coming under umbrella companies. Once a year, the International Franchisor Association has a convention. At that convention, we all come together and share best practices. The Dwyer Group enjoys a nice reputation of being a strong franchisor that knows what they are talking about. We listen, we learn and we share. It is a really great organization. In my 25 years of franchising, probably 40 to 50-percent of what I've learned in my early days, I learned by going to IFA events, and sitting across a round-table asking, why do you do this? Why do you do it that way? And we do the same. We share. It is a great place for growth and learning.

Julie Ann: That's great because you are going to help other companies do the same. I think what's important too, is that other people understand it is a journey. It's not something that's going to take a day. Again, with the repetition and reinforcement that you are so strong in so many ways, it speaks to the success of you creating this fabric of a large group of people from every level, and like you say, your corporate office, your franchisees and their employees as well. I think it is very commendable, Mary Thompson.

Mary: Well, it's a great group of people who all believe the same thing.

Julie Ann: So where do you go from here?

Mary: The thing we have to do is keep it front and center. As we get bigger, and as you mentioned at the beginning of the conversation that we have grown 100-percent in the last two years, that brings its set of own challenges. How not to lose your culture, and weaving the values through everything you do. A lot of my focus is making sure our growth is the right kind of growth and that we don't sacrifice who we are.

Julie Ann: Excellent. Do you have anything coming up on the horizon that you are implementing that is new?

Mary: We are excited because we just launched a new brand called Neighborly. We realized our homeowners have a great experience with Mr. Rooter, or Mr. Handyman, or Mr. Electric. They don't realize we are all sister companies, and we all follow the same set of Values and the core to who we are. So, we created this brand called Neighborly. After studying our customers, and talking to them, they said, "That's what we are looking for, the neighbor, somebody who can help us, a person who can help us maintain all things in our home." Now there is a place they can get all of their household needs in one place. We are just so excited about it.

Julie Ann: Brilliant! Then you probably just sit back and say, "Why did it take us so long?"

Mary:	I can't believe it took us so long! It was like one of those, Oh my, moments.
Julie Ann:	Aha! Definitely! So let's say we have a listener out there, and they haven't done any of this. Where do they start?
Mary:	The lawyer answer is it depends. It depends on the size of the company and what they want to get done. I would start with this. There is a good book called *The Powerful Engagement.* . . It's all about finding out what your true values are. What are the true values of your company? Keep them simple and straightforward. I would know those first, and get them written down. Then, find a way to talk about them and weave them into your day-to-day actions. Again, it's not your beliefs that make you a better person; it's your behavior. That's why we created an operational set of values. Like, responding in a timely fashion. I know what that means. I know what that looks like. That is something I can act on. So, something that is actionable, and not just, I'm going to be nice.
Julie Ann:	Thank you, Mary.
Mary:	Thank you, Julie Ann.
Julie Ann:	I know you are a very busy lady, and I really, really appreciate you taking time to share with us on Businesses that Care.

Favorite Food: It's a secret.

You might be sitting there right now and thinking, all that repetition is ridiculous, it sounds cult like. I understand I have heard that before. How can you argue with a 100-percent growth in the last two years? Seriously, think of what you do put into your day, every day. What are you reflecting in your workforce every day? Most of what is brewed in a working environment is subliminal. I personally like the fact that Mary and the Dwyer Group are walking the talk. As the quote at the beginning of the chapter says, they ask for accountability first, before asking others to be so. In my research I have found that respect works the same way. If you respect others, they are way more likely to respect you as well. The idea of, do what I say and not what I do is over. Only if you want to be successful will you need to be what you are looking for.

Another quote from Mary that is a vital notion to remember is, "It's not your beliefs that make you a better person, it's your behavior." It's your action that people look at as a validation of who you are as a human being. What do you want that to be?

It's the action you take or the inaction of the promises you make to a workforce that shows them how much you value each of them. What vision do you want them to have?

If repetition and reinforcement seem like dirty words to you, once they become the principles you live by, you can change your perception from negative to positive. It's your choice.

We live our
Code of Values by...

SHOWING **RESPECT** FOR
ALL PEOPLE

ACTING WITH **INTEGRITY** IN
ALL DEALINGS

SERVING **CUSTOMERS** WITH
ENTHUSIASM

& HAVING FUN IN THE PROCESS!

Friday Forward – Leadership and Beyond

with Robert Glazer, CEO, Acceleration Partners

"An A-player is right person, right seat, right time."
Robert Glazer

I WAS OVER THE MOON to talk with my guest, Robert Glazer, CEO of Acceleration Partners. I was stalking the Internet, doing research and reading through different articles on employee engagement/ experience and business culture. It's one way I stay so smart. I found an article in INC Magazine about a leader who was writing emails to his team called, Friday Forward. His workforce started to share it with others and it went viral. Now, over 40K people (as of 8/18) get Robert's Friday Forward email each week. Me included. Robert's posts are filled with the stories of his life. They are filled with honesty and vulnerability. Today's strongest leaders are authentic and transparent. They are real human beings that everyone can relate to. It makes a big difference in the way people work and their loyalty to a company.

It's a myth that millennials don't want to stay in a job. They will, if you are authentic, give them purpose and care. What a concept!

CONVERSATION WITH JULIE ANN AND ROBERT:

Julie Ann: Robert, you are part of a company called Acceleration Partners. Can you tell us a little bit about what the company is and what you do?

Robert: Sure, Acceleration Partners is a performance-marketing firm. We help a lot of large brands develop what I call affiliate marketing programs, which is a form of on-line marketing. It's sort of building a large pool of partners that work on behalf of the brand on a commission or a performance basis. So we build those programs for brands like Target', and Adidas', and Reebok', and help them acquire more customers online.

Julie Ann: That certainly seems like the type of business that is going to thrive. How did Friday Forward even pop into your head?

Robert: I always liked getting quotes, or stories, or articles about leadership and interesting stuff that always motivates me. I started to save them, and I'd see some sort of themes. One week I decided I'd start sending out a note to the team. I think I had a folder of these things that I had put together. I'd make a note about something, maybe link to a story, and then end with a quote. I started doing this, and I'd send them out on Friday mornings. It would be a "headed to the weekend" thing. Honestly, I didn't know if anyone was even reading them. What I realized in this process was that I was sort of writing my own little journal of inspiration, primarily for myself. I started to get emails back from employees saying, "I love this." "I look forward to these." "This was the perfect message this Friday." At some point, I was talking to some other business leaders' I'm in an organization called EO, and work with other business leaders around the US and globally. I told them, "You should try this I'll add you to my list, you can copy it or do your own, but it seems to have a really good impact." Then, they would write me back and say how our people love this, or I'm sending yours and they like it, or I'm doing my own. It just seemed like an opportunity. We live right now in a time where I think we are a little devoid of leadership. You look around at our leaders globally, and you see a lot of chaos and negative news, kind of autocratic and everyone is scaring everyone. It's just not what I understood as the job of a leader. After that, I said, you know, I wonder if other people would like these. So I started putting friends and family and other people on the list. It eventually just got too big to BCC everyone, and people were asking to sign up, so I switched to a sort of newsletter, where I tried to make a newsletter look as much like an email as I could. I stripped out everything, making it the cleanest I could. I couldn't manage subscribe, unsubscribe, and it just kept going. The article in INC has helped and some other stuff. It's grown almost to about 17 thousand people now (this was 12/2017, as of 1/2019 the number has grown to 100,000)) that are on weekly email.

Julie Ann: Were you a writer before you started doing this?

Robert: I wasn't a writer per say. I started writing and I wrote my first book in the last year. I started writing in a journal a few years ago. I've come to realize I enjoy writing and putting frameworks around things and listening to people's feedback about why something resonates. I kind of knew this, but it was put together in a framework that was easy for me to understand with some action around it. I get hundreds of notes every week from all over the world, and I write back to everyone. It keeps me writing every week, knowing the right message at the right time has an impact. Most every week, I get notes from people that say…

Julie Ann: Sometimes from me.

Robert: … "This is the best one yet." And it has nothing to do with the best one yet; it has to do where they were on that Friday. People have sent me really personal stories and responses without really knowing me. It's very interesting, and I keep a folder of them.

Julie Ann: It's very touching. I've done that before, too. And I think it's true for anytime you share a story or anytime you are talking about real life. I think everybody is going through something different at any moment in time. It's kind of like people saying I'm not going to tell you anything new today, I'm just going to say it in a different way, or you are going to be ready to receive it today. Right?

Robert: And the other thing you have going on, I think it was three or four weeks ago I alluded to this in a post, that social media is the top five percent of everyone's life and it is very curated. So if you are on this, what you see is all the wonderful stuff. People who have some bad stuff going on may be manicuring their perception that they are putting out there. You have some negativity, a lot of negativity and false positivity, but I don't think you have a lot of just authenticity. People say honestly, I like authenticity and vulnerability, or transparency. People are transparently not honest.

Julie Ann: I like that.

Robert: I just like people who are consistent. I can get along with a wide range of different types of people. If I know this guy is an embellisher, and he's always an embellisher, and he is aware of it, then I'm good with that. It's when people say one thing and do another, and pretend to be different. Integrity is tricky. We all say that we know it. I've been exposed to a lot of global leadership stuff, and there are a lot of cultural issues around integrity. What one person would consider integral in one place is just not in another place. I think transparency is sometimes a little more accurate.

Julie Ann: I think you hit it too, when you said being authentic. When you are authentic, that's what really comes through to people. That's what people connect to. If you share that your dog died, and how sad you are, that there is a void in your life, like when you come in the house and it's quiet, other people who have had pets can relate to that, right? It is a connection with people.

Robert: People want to share. I constantly see this in small groups. They want to share and be more authentic and vulnerable. There's an exercise called, "A Life Line." It is used a lot in small groups. We've done this in some leadership programs at our company. Usually a member of the leadership team is in the group and will go first. They will lay out their life story–in a graph plotted out with highs and lows. Whoever goes first sets the tone for the entire group. People have shared some incredible stuff because they were surprised at what I was willing to share about my life, or what others were willing to share about their lives. But if it started off shallow, then everyone's contribution would be shallow. We purposely started our sessions off deeper. I remember one session where two people made a connection about a bad experience each had in their lives, which was almost identical. They work together every day, yet they would not have known that otherwise.

Julie Ann: Right. It's true. If one person is willing to be open and more vulnerable, it makes it easier for others to do the same.

Robert: A facilitator shared with me what he does in a group. He goes around and asks, "What's something bad that happened to you this month?" In the first round he says, "I lost something, whatever that might be." Then, they all go around and share. In the second round, he says, "I found out my wife is cheating on me." And he said it is unbelievable.

Julie Ann: What everyone else is willing to say then.

Robert: Versus the first round.

Julie Ann: That's great. I love that you are willing to do that. What about your *own* team? What has been the reaction from them regarding Friday Forward?

Robert: They are very supportive. I get comments each week. I still write it as if I am writing it to *my* team and sort of sharing a story. They are very supportive, and I will hear back in the same way about certain posts. I may have referenced it. A lot of it ties to my personal core values, which are also very intertwined into our company's core values and a lot of our operating principles. I think a lot of the teams are familiar, and they tend to support some of the stuff we are trying to practice and that we show encouragement on a regular basis.

Julie Ann: Have you seen a change in your company's culture since you started doing that?

Robert: Yes. We really doubled down on our culture, I think two years ago, and re-looked at our hiring process, and sort of narrowed our core values. It was about the same time I started the Friday Forward emails. It's hard to isolate that. I think it's had an impact on some of the people that leave. It's how we stay in touch and remain connected. It's tied to a program we have, called "Mindful Transition," about having a totally open transition process when people think it's time to move on or we think it's time for them to move on. We are trying to eliminate the two-week notice thing. Which I think is terrible for companies and terrible for those moving on.

Julie Ann: And most of them now don't have two weeks. It is more like, "Oh, good morning. You will be escorted to your office now, and you are out."

Robert: We are the opposite of that and it has taken a lot of practice. If you are not happy, start the discussion of let's work on a transition plan or let's help you find a job. We are a very performance-oriented culture. But I think looking at performance objectively, yet really rooting for people as human beings. We are able to have a discussion that hey, we are really rooting for you to do better, and we will help, but this is not the role for you. And, we need to find you a better role. We have only really walked one person to the door in the same day that I can remember, in our company's history and that was over an integrity issue. I was very influenced by Patty McCord and Netflix and all the work she did on their culture. If you are just respectful to people and tell them the truth, they can handle it. Truth and respect go hand in hand. A lot of times, and where some fail as leaders, when someone is leaving, they are leaving because they found a better opportunity, or they are moving, and we can't get over being left. So we feel the need to lash out against them, and I just think that makes no sense. It is a small world, it is a social-media world, we are all tied together, and we have really good relationships with those who used to work here.

Julie Ann: You don't know which of those alumni are going to be your next customer.

Robert: Right. And some of them have been or have referred people. I think we need to be more like sports teams. In sports, when contracts are up, they change teams all the time, there's no animosity. You finish playing and everyone knows you are going to be a free agent and you are going somewhere else next year. There is something about the paradigm that has developed around this at work. I do understand that this is because of how some of the companies behave that they think the better option is for everyone to lie. For the employer not to give honest feedback, and the employee to have lots of doctors' appointments....

Julie Ann: While they are really going to interviews.

Robert: ...rather than starting a discussion. I think the two-weeks' notice is terrible. It is bad for us and it's bad for the client. It's also that the person tells me they have been happy, then I realize every doctor's appointment they had was really going to an interview. Now, my last memory of them is not great. It's a small world, too in terms of performance reviews. When we are hiring someone, we barely check the references they give us. It's very easy to find out where they worked and who they worked with by back channel. So, I think for candidates too, it tends to burn a bridge. Yet, I do understand why some of them do that because in their culture, if they started that discussion, they'd be walked out the door that day. So we have taken that off the table. We say, look, we will never do that if you come to us and have an honest discussion. We will figure out something that is good for everyone and do that over a period of time.

Julie Ann: Well, I think a lot of times, the "rules" that came from somewhere, were set up and all one way. People are told when they leave a job, not to burn that bridge. Now what's happening for the companies that really understand what is going on out there, the rule of don't burn your bridges is for the employer as well. There are more cultures being created where they are having this discussion because somebody may not be a good fit for you. Probably one of the best mentors taught me the phrase…It's not a good fit. Then it's not personal, it is just not a good fit. But that person who is not a good fit, who finds someplace else that is a better fit can still refer clients and good employees to you later and vice versa. Maybe they will work someplace or in a different business that you can refer to. So instead of burning bridges, you are working together to make sure everything is a good fit for everyone. The other side is that sometimes you have a very good employee that comes into one department, but aren't good in that department, but maybe they'd be good in another department. So why get rid of a good employee because maybe they came into sales, but they are better in marketing.

Robert: We have a phrase we borrowed that an A-player is right person, right seat, right time. And the right time comes in because we are a high growth company. We have been growing 30 to 40 percent for several years. When you do that your needs are constantly changing. It's very different than a company that is not growing or only growing 4 or 5 percent, where the jobs are pretty much the same. Just the right person is non-negotiable. If they don't have the core values, they are gone. They leave or we manage them out. We don't tolerate the brilliant jerk. Some cultures do. If they are the right person, they may be in the wrong seat, as you said, and we have had some examples. Again, starting that discussion–this isn't working. Gee, this is the right person, but they are just doing the wrong thing, in the wrong seat. We move them to another role, and they thrive and it is great. We add the right time in because one of the things that are hard for people to identify is that when someone is the right person, right seat six months ago, the needs of that seat may have changed dramatically and suddenly, they don't fit anymore. Perhaps the role has become bigger, they may need to step aside to make way for someone else, but often can't do that. It is a constant evolution for us. We can't leave it alone. You don't really go from the right person, to not the right person, but is the seat right and are we getting the outcomes we need? Just because one person was an A-player last year in that role, that role may have totally different things that it needs right now. We have to have that process. When we talk about an A-player, we are very clear that it is not a fixed mindset. It's not here is an A-player and here is a C-player. It is not that they are not an A-player in our system anymore and they need to go somewhere else. When Patty McCord at Netflix, talked to people, she would tell them they are not going to be successful in this role. You don't want to fail, and I don't want you to fail. People know when they are not doing well. Success for everyone is in helping them find something they would be better at.

Julie Ann: That evolution, that journey, and that realization that the journey is going on is part of the new cultures I am bringing into Businesses That Care. They understand they are not going to stick somebody in a job for 15 years doing the same thing. Our businesses are changing so fast, and you want growth, and with growth comes change. It is time to recognize that. For instance, the idea of the annual performance review is just a joke, right. I see you giggle there. Anyone who has a culture that really wants to thrive is no longer doing that because flourishing is a constant journey.

Robert: We do a quarterly check-in, but we make a big point of actual feedback in real time. There was training for Ritz Carlton on their sort of customer service methodology. They said they have a rule, and we sort of adopted this, of 72 hours. Either give people feedback on something in 72 hours or you have to let it go. What they said is, and it was so clear when the guy explained it, you sit there in a quarterly review 90 days later with all these grievances that you have built up, and they call it targeting. The person feels like, "Are you kidding me? You have been saving this list of stuff that's bothering you from three months ago?" That's not about improving the problem, that's sort of feeling better about you and evening the score. Feedback is about improving. If there is a problem with how a call went, tell me after so I can do the next one better.

Julie Ann: I've told this story several times; I'm a former accountant and in one of my first accounting jobs, the owner of a small office didn't like something I was doing. But he let me do it all tax season long. Of course, at the end, he was really ticked off, stewing. He never gave the work back to me to correct, he was doing it for three months. So, when we had my annual review and he expressed how frustrated he was, I was old enough and bold enough to say why didn't you tell me on day one. You never gave me a chance to get better. And you've been angry about this for three months? That's not fair to me.

Robert: The feedback process is continuous. There are quarterly goals. Each quarter there is a 30-minute conversation where we check in, do re-calibration, and there is no annual review. I think they are quickly becoming extinct from what I have seen.

Julie Ann: We are already experiencing a shortage of employees. It is only the companies that have opened their eyes and ears and souls to this changing employee experience that are going to be able to keep anyone. Personally, I think there will be many businesses that shut down because they are not going to have the people they need to deliver their products and services.

Robert: A friend of mine runs a company that constantly wins one of the top places to work. He is sort of a champion of millennials. It's a top performing company, where the people work pretty hard. He said to me in a conversation that he is really trying to communicate to people that if they don't entice or excite this generation of people to want to work in their business, they will just go to work for themselves. I don't think people will realize the existential threat of not having enough employees.

People are not going to work in a place where they don't understand the purpose.

Julie Ann: It is a very real threat. Besides having a huge population retiring, you have a smaller population coming into the workplace, and what you said is key. We have a lot more individuals becoming entrepreneurs. There are degrees they can get in entrepreneurship, and that didn't exist 20 years ago. So that combination is going to make it really important. It sounds to me that you are definitely on the right path for that.

If people want to join in on the Friday Forward phenomenon, go here - Fridayfwd.com. For those who think they could never write like that, the more you read what someone else has, the more you realize you can do it too.

Robert: I see some companies have a slack channel to distribute Friday Forward and it has the same impact. They appreciate that their CEO shared it with them. So you get credit for sharing it, even if you don't want to do your own writing.

Julie Ann: That's great! I am so glad you joined us today. It has been interesting and enlightening, and you've given more than one great idea for our listeners to use in their own companies. So thank you Robert, so much.

Robert: Thank you. If you google Friday Forward, you will find it or it is Fridayfwd.com and you can sign up for it and get next Friday's message.

Julie Ann: I highly recommend that. Until next time, this is Julie Ann Sullivan saying thank you for being here. Go ahead and use everything you read in this chapter and create your own Simple Solutions for Great Results.

Favorite Food – Good BBQ

Robert Glazer is truly a visionary. He is not afraid to be honest, transparent or try new ideas.

He is a shining example of what it means to walk the talk. His business understands that each employee is unique. Every step of their journey within the organization is important, from onboarding, to their ongoing authentic communication, to exit. Even the words they use make a difference. They have quarterly conversations, not reviews. Robert understands that the smallest nuances in how you speak and treat your employees can create a business culture that flourishes on a personal and professional level. The company's growth is in direct proportion to the growth of its workforce. Isn't that what you want?

Walking in Wisdom and The G.R.O.W. Theory

with Jeff McManus, Director, University of Mississippi

"You can't plant seeds and get the fruit the next day."

Jeff McManus

I HAVE TO BE HONEST. When an agent from Interview Valet approached me to interview Jeff McManus, I was a little skeptical. I really couldn't imagine what the director of landscape services from Ole Mis could add to my audience. Being one who teaches others to be open minded, I took my own advice and learned more. I loved when I received information about Jeff's working philosophy. He wanted to have people not just work for a pension and a paycheck, he wanted them to work for passion and purpose. I'm a big believer in the importance of purpose, so that got my attention. After hearing about Jeff's G.R.O.W. theory, I was impressed. The clincher was the title of his book, Growing Weeders Into Leaders. Honestly, this interview with Jeff McManus blew my socks off. He is wise and one of the most caring individuals I have had the privilege to interview. He has become a client and a friend. This is what happens when you are open to new ideas and perspectives. Jeff McManus has been doing this for 17 years, and you might be wondering what he can teach you? Let me tell you, no matter what industry you are in, Jeff has got a lot of valuable knowledge to share. Here we go...

CONVERSATION WITH JULIE ANN AND JEFF:

Julie Ann: You are a busy guy, Jeff. Thank you so much for joining us today.

Jeff: Julie Ann, I am excited to be on the podcast with you.

Julie Ann: I like that you are excited. Let's talk a little bit about Grow Theory. Where did it come from, first of all?

Jeff: Grow Theory is my management style. I was talking about it, with a very smart lady whom I work with, JoAnn Edwards. She is a coach. As we kept talking, she kind of drew these things out on a napkin. She told me, "This is what it sounds like you are doing." It was like a roadmap. She brought clarity to what I am doing.

Julie Ann: That is what good coaches do.

Jeff: Absolutely! She is well worth it. JoAnn just made that crystal clear for me. She gave me the acronym G.R.O.W., which is easy for this old boy to understand and always remember. That's what I like, simplicity. Keep it simple so all of us can understand. It's not something that I always talk about with our people. This is something I do, it's modeling and the way I manage people. Real quick, G is for greatness. Everything that we do is built toward a greater purpose. It matters, it is important. The job's position, no matter what the job is, it is very important. You want people to know they are important to the organization.

The R is the Resiliency. Julie Ann, all of us are going to have problems. We are all going to have challenges, but do we have a culture that can persist and push through and work together as a team? When we have calamities, like we have had many hurricanes, people will pull together. But in the workplace, you don't always see that. Sometimes in the workplace what we see is people building silos, and working against each other, and undermining one another. But how do we build that resiliency and that culture of working together? It is a big part of what we do. One of our sayings is, We Adapt and Overcome. We need that mindset.

Julie Ann: Silos are definitely culture killers in any business.

Jeff: They really are. This resiliency helps break down those silos and that mentality. We look to the military because they have a good model. They don't pay their people that much money on the front lines, yet they have this great attitude of adapting and overcoming in any circumstance.

The O is for Opportunity. What opportunities are around us? You know opportunities often look like a problem, they really do. They come dressed like a big old problem. I found that it is much better to get more people around the room, around the table, around the tailgate, to talk about problems and try to get the best solution. Sometimes that solution doesn't work, but it is a failure and it is the manure we keep growing in!

Julie Ann: Ha, ha, ha. You have to have it!

Jeff: And the W is the key for us. This is probably the most important one that I started doing about six years ago. It is Walking our team in Wisdom. That is taking a moment out of every month to stop and listen and talk. A lot of times we will bring in a speaker, maybe it is DVD, maybe it is live, and we use that to springboard conversation. We had a speaker one time, talk about the word, Adaptability. We spent that time talking about adaptability. It is amazing how the culture has changed over the last six years as we continually talk about values, principles, listen to Ted Talks, and then let our folks have conversations. My job is, as a facilitator, to get those conversations going because I want people to grow on the inside. I want them to be continually seeking and growing.

Julie Ann: That's really interesting because a lot of companies will watch a Ted Talk, then everybody leaves and there is no discussion. It's better to have a discussion and talk about what best practices you will put forward. As people share with one another, one person at one end of the table perhaps forgot about what a person at the other end of the table learned. So those discussions are so important. I'm sitting here thinking, greatness, resilience, purpose; I'm all about that. Finding Opportunity in Change was the first title for my Change Management presentation. It's not if change will happen, it is when, and how often. It is just the way life is. If we have a mindset to find opportunities, that's great. I love the idea that you come up with a solution, and hey, that solution may or may not work. A lot of times we don't know until we try it, but if you have the mindset to try it and see how it works, as opposed to this must work and if it doesn't, it is a failure. No, it's another opportunity to tweak it and grow. So grow, there you go.

Jeff: Yes, there you go. The biggest honor for somebody in a leadership position is when your staff is doing things you no longer have to be a part of, which you no longer have to help make it happen. I've been amazed, as we have created this landscape university where we are training our staffs and bringing people up. Our staff is actually creating the classes. I'm amazed at how much that has evolved, and how much better they have gotten since we originally started six years ago. I'm like, holy cow, I'm not even here anymore, and this thing has gotten so much better. I've sort of gotten out of the way. Good thing I have good, strong self-esteem, and I can handle it.

Julie Ann: And isn't that what great leaders are all about? Being able to get out of the way and let people grow. A great leader isn't someone who says, follow me, do me, be me, and serve me. They are more of a how can I help you grow.

Jeff: Tom Peter's said, "Leaders don't create followers, they create more leaders." And that has been the key to our success, empower people to continually grow into the mental aspect that they are a leader. They may not lead a lot of people, but they lead themselves, and that totally affects our whole organization. If they lead themselves well, then, they come in with a positive attitude, they are on time, they are solution-oriented, they are always looking for ways that we can be better, they look for that extra-mile service, the how can we take care of you? Now, we have the right mindset. Those are the kind of people we try to attract to our organization.

Julie Ann: It is interesting because the quality of their work is higher, too. It's funny you said that's the kind of people you try to attract. One of the outcomes of these podcasts, Businesses That Care, is businesses have been putting these on their websites so when they recruit, they have people listen to it.

Jeff: So smart.

Julie Ann: People know right away if that's the culture they want to be a part of. In the interview process, the people will ask questions about the podcast, and when you heard this, what did that mean to you, or how did that fit for you? I just got an email from someone who was on a previous podcast for Businesses That Care, and they said they recruited for a really tough position to fill, and when they asked that person why they applied, they said it was because of the Businesses That Care podcast. They knew it was the culture they wanted to be in.

Jeff: That is great. Disney, Ritz-Carlton, and some of these bigger organizations have that figured out. It's exactly what you are talking about. Seeing if it is a good fit in the beginning. What a disservice we can do to our potential employees by hiring the wrong person. If they are not a good fit, it's like planting a shrub in an area where the grass should be.

Julie Ann: Or putting a square in a circle.

Jeff: Right.

Julie Ann: Or putting a shade plant in the full sun.

Jeff: That's right. You can plant it, but it just doesn't work. It gets burned up.

Julie Ann: You talked about your monthly meetings where you have to bring people in, and either have a speaker or facilitate a conversation or both. What else do you do that allows your workforce to grow?

Jeff: A small thing . . . We have department meetings, and I used to lead the department meetings every week. Then, I realized I needed to grow leaders, and I took a playbook out of Toastmasters. I began to set our meetings up and let our people lead them. We'd develop a written agenda, so we have probably 10 people talking in our meetings and giving updates. We have our staff members leading the meetings. So everybody in our department leads a meeting at least once a year, sometimes maybe twice. Also, we do a teaching part where we talk about plants.

Not all of our staff knows a lot about plants, believe it or not. We will have a plant for the week; this week we may talk about an azalea, or we may talk about a certain type of weed. Setting up the meetings like this causes them to learn that the teacher learns as much or more than the student. Then, we have a safety part, maybe a two-minute part, and another person does that. We are letting our people have a voice in the meeting, and talk a spell, and participate.

Julie Ann: And that engages them.

Jeff: Engages them, absolutely. Everybody gets a calendar; we make our own custom calendars. They bring their calendar and an ink pen to every meeting so they can take notes. We have critical dates where we have functions on a big campus, and everybody needs to know that. It is a huge communication, a great facilitator for us where questions are asked. We have an Apple TV so I can throw things quickly up on the TV as somebody talks about something, I can look it up, and then throw it up. We do a lot of that and at the end we do a little motivational video. Typically, I will go to Facebook or somewhere and take a 2 to 5 minute video about core values. We will watch that for inspiration, and maybe talk about it for a few minutes. At the very end of the meeting, we do stretching, and then we read our Landscape Creed. The Landscape Creed is a creed that our team developed. We ask two questions when we developed this, first, what do you want to be known for? Second, what do you want the new person who comes to work for you to know about landscape services? We talk about some of those values briefly to remind us. We read the Landscape Creed together and have a little one, two, three, team! Then we go do our deal. I think those little things may seem like little quirky things, but having those things together helps solidify our unity and our culture as well.

Julie Ann: That's right. I think that it is important in a break room, for example, to know what kind of magazines are in there, and what is on the TV? If news is running all the time, it's not really motivating, it certainly is not finding commonalities among people because people are going to have different opinions. What if you just ran Ted Talks and motivational videos and funny videos?

One thing I want to ask you is when you bring people into the fold, so to speak, there's got to be people who come on and say, "Oh, my gosh you are kidding me, no one runs a landscaping department like this." They never experienced anything like it. They have just been "laborers," told to do this, and go do that. That's what the communication is like. Have you had any experience where someone has come to you and said, "Jeff, I didn't know what this was at first, but I feel like I've found nirvana!"

Jeff: What I have are people smiling, and those that come and shake my hand and say, "I love doing this, thank you for hiring me."

That's happened a lot. It shows me we have hired the right people. Usually, the ones that have a negative attitude or are complainers typically don't make it through the interview process. We try to talk people out of working for us. We tell them how bad it is, and we don't sugarcoat it. You are going to tend to animals the rest of your life; somebody's got to pick it up. You are going to be picking up trash, you never graduate from that. I'm out there picking up trash, that's how we lead by example. We look for the mindset of the person who wants to do that, who wants to be behind the scenes and make others successful. We look for people who want to make the university successful. We want to make athletics, academics, everything successful. Those people who are attracted to that and fill those core values will embrace what I believe. We want them to feel like, "I'm home and I love this." We are doing hot, thankless things every day. When I say hot, in Mississippi it gets hot! It is hot and dirty! Not everybody can do this anymore in America. I often tell our folks that we are doing things most people can't do anymore and most people don't want to do. We try to make sure they know it is a greatness building them up for what they do.

Julie Ann: It seems to me that you make them feel an intricate part of the bigger picture. So when the University of Mississippi wins a football game, they were a part of that too.

Jeff: That's right. Every Monday morning, we bring in speakers. We bring our coaches in, people from the academic world, anybody we can get to tell the message of how important they are and what they are a part of. I want our staff, not only to hear it, but here's the kicker for us, I want our staff to be asking questions. I want them to engage in conversation with these people who are successful. What kind of questions do you ask a successful person? Can you approach a person who is making a million dollars to have an intelligent conversation with them? You don't ask a person like that some weird question, like how much money do you make? You ask them what books they are reading, or how did you get to where you are? What inspires you? What habits do you attribute to your success? That's what we are teaching our team–how to be a student of success, and how to listen. We also teach our folks that they are mentors to these students who come and work for us. Who knows if in ten years, one of these students may come back and say it was you Mr. landscaper who changed my life.

Julie Ann: Absolutely, it happens all the time. You are making them students of life, which I really like. For many of these people who come in, especially the students, maybe they never felt they could ask questions. Of course, the people who can ask the most intelligent questions are the ones who grow the most, as far as I'm concerned.

Jeff: Yeah. You've got to be willing to get in the game.

Julie Ann: Whatever the game is.

Jeff: That's right. If it is Q and A, and you are too shy or bashful, life is going to pass you by. So, get in the game and ask questions.

Julie Ann: How do you think this has benefitted, not only the people who work for you, but the college and the community? Not just the work you do, because that is obvious, people come and love what they see and feel they are in a good environment. What do you think it has done to the mindset of the people who work for you, and the university, and your community?

Jeff: Well, I think our team has set a great example for others to look up to. They get compliments all the time. I had this happen to me several times where our staff has come to my office, asked to talk to me, and said, look, some of these things we are doing, I know you want our team to get better egos. I want to share this personal thing with you, This Walking in Wisdom, the classes, the stuff we are learning, it works at home. My wife and I were going to get a divorce, and we aren't getting a divorce anymore because the things I learned helped me change. I realized it wasn't my wife that was the problem. I realized a lot of it was myself.

Julie Ann: Well, I have a couple of people to send your way!

Jeff: You know, Julie Ann, it is self-awareness.

Julie Ann: You can never have too much, that's my motto.

Jeff: We have blind spots, we all do. And when you can see those for the first time, and you realize that, you can save yourself a lot of heartache. And another guy told me he was about to break up with his fiancée, and the Walking in Wisdom leader class had helped him as well to take on a whole new perspective. That has helped our team with not pointing the finger at other people as being the problem, and taking ownership and responsibility. That's half our issues. We have got to own it, and we've got to own the decisions we make and that's been beneficial.

Julie Ann: Everything you say resonates with me. When I talk about employee engagement, I talk about blame. One of the things I say is why don't you take ten minutes in your day and look at you, instead of looking at other people. When I talk to people about collaboration, it's about what it is about you that doesn't get along with that bully, or that person who is self-righteous, or whatever it is about them that bugs you. What is it about you that is stopping you from working with them? We really can't change other people, right? They need to be able to change for themselves. Self-awareness is key. I've always said if you can't see it, you can't change it.

Jeff: Right. And you can lead the horse to water . . .

Julie Ann:	But you can never make them drink.
Jeff:	I try to make them really thirsty! Hopefully, they will drink. But it comes down to the person wanting to see it, and change it, and it's not always easy.
Julie Ann:	You're showing them a lit path. That's what you are doing. And that's what people want to have–an exemplary workplace culture. People like you are creating these lit paths. Then, it is up to the individuals to walk down those paths or not, to be able to see the opportunities on those paths. The other side of that is if they don't, it doesn't make them a bad person, they just aren't a good fit for that culture.
Jeff:	That's right. Eventually, they will either move along or go to another culture. A lot of the guys, who are kind of on the fence, came in and have grown tremendously. One of the things we do is take our staff to the local library. Why? Well, you know, reading or listening to books changes your life, and it's free! We like that word free. I have several staff members who are reading leadership books now who weren't before. You can't go wrong when people are doing things like that.
Julie Ann:	You give them the opportunity to see that it is available because a lot of people just don't know. I can tell you the best trips I took with my son when he was 10 or 12 was when we got into the car and drove for days and listened to Gulliver's Travels, or Tom Sawyer on CD in the car. Again, you are teaching them something that can further their career, but can also further their lives, as well as enhance their lives with their families.
	Well, I do not want to run out of time before we at least talk a little bit about your book.

Jeff: Well, thank you Julie Ann. My book is called *Growing Weeders into Leaders: Leadership Lessons from the Ground Level.* It's a little bit of the story of changing a culture. I took on a very negative, toxic culture in a government environment where you can't just come in and fire people.

Julie Ann: You can't clean house.

Jeff: You can't. I had to build relationships, and it was a long road. It's like planting crops. You can't plant seeds and get the fruit the next day. You've got to wait and be patient. And now it's 17 years later, and I'm enjoying a lot of the fruit that was planted early on and a lot of the plowing and breaking up the fertile ground. This book is a little bit of that, and it's also a lot about leadership lessons that we are applying that have made us successful. We have won five national awards. We call them national championships here, for the most beautiful campus. We think we have taken some average people and turned them into superstars as far as landscaping is concerned. We share a lot of those secrets in the book. They are not gardening secrets, they are leadership principles.

Julie Ann: I love that you use your work as a metaphor for growing people. It fits so well, doesn't it? I read a story once, and it was about a seed and how difficult it is for a seed to move through rock and earth and be plummeted with rain and how difficult just emerging is. And once it emerges, you still have to be patient, but it grows much faster. I know I can get to the light and find that there is a path, but getting to that path is tougher than once you hit the path.

Jeff: Right. It's all in the process and it is the patience, the process, and the watering. You need three things when you grow really good grass: sunlight, water, and food.

When you think about it, that's what we need too. When you feed grass, you only feed it once or twice during the springtime. We need those meals, that nutrition, those people speaking into our lives that water, that refreshment/nourishment that we need every day. Then, we need that sunlight, that warmth, we need something to be attracted to, that vision. So those people are attracted to the vision of what we are doing. We have purpose, and that's what the sunlight is.

Julie Ann: Jeff, I want to thank you for being with us today. It has been illuminating, and very fruitful.

Jeff: Love it. Thank you, Julie Ann, for letting me share a little of our story with your audience today.

Favorite Food - Mexican

Maybe it was his Mississippi accent or his southern generous spirit, but I got done with this interview and just sighed. Jeff's fundamental wisdom about how to treat people was so simple and magnanimous. He has perfected how to nurture success in the people that work with him and yet, get out of their way. Jeff is a perfect example of how a leader can earn trust by trusting and how to earn respect by being respectful.

Jeff McManus is certainly a gift to everyone who comes into his life. He is in a perfect profession because he is the ultimate nurturer. He's no pushover, but his dedication to the growth of his workers is exemplary. Wow! That is what I felt then and how I feel now. This was a gift in my life and I hope in yours as well.

Here is the Landscape Creed from the University of Mississippi:

LANDSCAPERS CREED

WE, THE DEPARTMENT OF LANDSCAPE SERVICE, ARE A
TEAM OF HARD WORKING INDIVIDUALS UNITED
UNDER
ONE BANNER AND DEDICATED TO INSPIRING OTHERS.
WE…
LEAD BY EXAMPLE.
ADAPT AND OVERCOME.
NEVER STOP TRAINING AND GROWING.
DEDICATE OURSELVES TO PROFESSIONAL INTEGRITY.
SERVE WITH RESPECT AND PRIDE.
CULTIVATE GREATNESS.
ACHIEVE QUALITY RESULTS WITH AN EYE FOR DETAIL.
PROMOTE AND PROVIDE A BEAUTIFUL ENVIRONMENT.
EXCEL THROUGH HIGH STANDARDS AND EXCELLENCE
WITHIN.
I AM A LANDSCAPE REBEL.

Focus on Serving

with Larry Sutton, President, RNR Tire Express

"To really be a great leader is to shut up and listen."
Larry Sutton

M Y FIRST THOUGHT WAS, "What can a tire and wheel franchisor from Oklahoma teach me and my audience about creating a superior company culture?" A biased and unfair thought? Absolutely. However, I am pretty good at getting out of my own way and always wanting to learn about a new business, Larry's wheel and tire company intrigued me. We had a pre-podcast chat and I was sold. His voice alone made me excited for our interview and his sense of humor and humility sealed the deal.

Larry Sutton is the Founder and President of RNR Tire Express. He started as a little guy with one store in 2000, and now he has 117 franchises across the United States. Larry's background is from humble beginnings and not always the easiest of households. He became a successful entrepreneur and retired early in his 40's. Instead of this leading to a happy life, he was bored. He took the time to search for an idea that invigorated him. Through trial and error, due to diligence and the ability to take a chance, he found what was missing in his life. He is passionate, open to new ideas and a real character. You will really enjoy Larry's self-deprecating humor. It is just one of the reasons I chose this podcast episode for this book.

CONVERSATION WITH JULIE ANN AND LARRY:

Larry: Good morning, Julie Ann, how are you? I appreciate you having me on.

Julie Ann: I'm great! And where are you? Florida?

Larry: Tampa, Florida, which normally would be very warm at this time of year. We seldom ever get a cold front, but this week has been cold for us. In our neck of the woods, cold is like 60 degrees.

Julie Ann: There's a cold front here too, but it's 20 degrees. I'm not feeling too bad for you.

Have you always lived in the Tampa area?

Larry: No, ma'am. I was born and raised in Oklahoma.

Julie Ann: That's where that accent I hear comes from.

Larry: Yes, that Texas kicker at the end of the voice. I came to Florida very early. My mother was a single mom, and she came to Florida when I was going into high school to go to work for her brother, who was an entrepreneur. And that's what brought us to Florida, and I've been here ever since.

Julie Ann: And what made you open up a tire store? Kids don't usually grow up and say, "Someday I want to own a tire store."

Larry: Exactly. Well, interestingly, it is a longer story than we have time for. I had another business that I had started and was very successful with. I had 30 stores in the traditional rent-to-own business, which is televisions, appliances, and things like that. We had built 150-store chain across the Southeastern United States. We actually sold that in 1997, to a company that was doing a lot of mergers and wanting to go public. So I kind of went into an early retirement, and I was in my late 40s, thinking I was going to do what I thought I wanted to do, which was play golf all the time. Then, when I started doing that I found out that it actually wasn't really what I wanted to do. So, after a year I was bored to tears.

Julie Ann: That happens a lot. People think early retirement will be great! Then it becomes, what do I do?

Larry: It was horrible. I guess some people are built for it, and some people aren't. In my case, I was just a miserable soul. And I didn't know what I was missing, but I knew I was missing something. And much later, I figured out it was the interaction with people, watching people grow and learn, and me learning myself about new things. All of that, all of a sudden was missing in my life, and I didn't know it. Getting up and playing golf after a while, just became a boring life. So I decided to look around and try a few different things. Actually, of all things, I bought a bunch of smoothie franchises and got into the smoothie business. I found myself at 49 years old out on the street in Jacksonville, Florida, dressed as a banana giving away free smoothie samples.

Julie Ann: I want a picture of that!

Larry: I had two of my kids with me, dressed as fruits, and of course they said, "Dad, this is not what we want to be doing." So, that didn't work out because it didn't fit what I was missing, it wasn't the solution.

Julie Ann: I bet your kids were happy that didn't work out.

Larry: Absolutely. So I tried a few different things, invested in a few businesses, but still nothing had really clicked. A friend of mine had mentioned there was somebody out in Texas trying a new thing with tires…tires on payments, as opposed to just going in and paying cash. And, of course, I had experience in the payment business. I thought that was something worth looking into. I flew out to take a look. And one thing inherently true about entrepreneurs is that for some reason, rightfully or wrongfully, we believe we can do something better than what we see. Of course that was me at the time. I saw this had some possibilities, but they were doing it wrong; so let me try something different. I came back and did a little research in the industry, and at that time, it really wasn't about tires, it was about custom wheels. What these guys were really doing was big fancy wheels. The only reason tires were involved is because they had to put tires on the wheels when they were putting them out there. I did research, and I went to Vegas to a trade show to find out more about the wheel and tire industry. It certainly appeared that there was a bubble occurring. When you looked at the total amount of after-market wheel sales in the country and you tracked it, it looked like it was on a continuous up. So, I thought, well, let me try it. I came up with a name and a concept, and six months later we opened a store. We couldn't spell tires, but we were in the tire business.

Julie Ann: From that one store you have gone to 117 franchises across the country. From my research in talking to other franchisors, one of the most important pieces of having franchises is that you want them all to do business the way you meant business to be done.

Larry: Yes, ma'am.

Julie Ann: So there's quite a bit of making sure that if you go to an RNR Tire Express in California, it looks like RNR Tire Express in Tampa right?

Larry: Correct. Yes. I had to learn that the hard way. It was not my intention to be a franchiser. I had three or four stores open and they were very successful. And I had a reputation in the business, so people started to come to look and see what I was doing. A gentleman came and looked for a few days, and said he wanted to do this. I said, fine go ahead. He said, no, you don't understand. I want to do the same, exact thing, blah blah . . . And I said go ahead. He said no, you don't get it. I want to do everything you are doing . . .

Julie Ann: Did he become the head of your franchising department?

Larry: No, he was my first franchisee. And God bless his soul, he has since passed away. But I am sure he is looking down going what did I start? Anyway, that worked and before you know it, someone else came along, and it's funny you mentioned that. One of my attorneys told me early on, he said, Larry, you are a pretty great guy, but I don't think you are going to be a good franchiser. I asked him why, and he said because you don't know how to say no. And to be quite frank with you, we had to learn the hard way that there are some things as a franchiser you do have to say no to.

Julie Ann: Is that where the Yes CEO mentality came from that I hear so much about?

Larry: Probably. My inherent belief is that people who have that entrepreneurial spirit are very creative and very imaginative. Left alone with their own thoughts, they will come up with some great ideas. My fear was holding that back from the guys. I had to find that balance between there are some things you can't change, and here's who we need to be. By the same token, if you have ideas on how to make this company better and it would benefit everyone, go ahead and try it and see if it works. So we are kind of an unusual franchise in the sense that we don't believe we have all the good ideas. We believe it is our responsibility to allow people to think a little bit outside the box. We are the collector of the ideas, and then we let people Beta site, or we'll Beta site the idea. If it works, then we bring it in and give it to everybody. As long as it is not going to hurt our brand, I am open-minded and say, why not, let's give it a shot. Because some of the most effective things we do, including our brand that we go by right now, actually came from allowing a franchise to try something new.

Julie Ann: I couldn't agree with you more, that great leaders are partially great leaders because they are able to let go and allow people to not only come up with ideas, but you have opened the door to allowing them to bring up the ideas and try them out. There are a lot of places where people work where they have ideas but are too afraid to bring them forward.

Larry: Some places don't exist with open arms.

Julie Ann: Right. So you are trying it out to find out whether it works. And if it works, you can say that was a great idea, and we tried it. If it doesn't prove to be viable, then here are what the stumbling blocks were.

Larry: Exactly.

Julie Ann: So that person now feels very valued, very acknowledged, and very appreciated, even if it doesn't work.

Larry: Exactly. Because they got to try, and if they don't try or if you shut it down, there will always be the, "what if that would have worked."

Julie Ann: Why didn't they listen? Why didn't they at least try?

Larry: And Julie Ann, it really goes beyond the franchisee, it actually goes all the way down in your hierarchy of folks, to the lowest of those because they have ideas too. Shop technicians who are putting on the tires and wheels . . .

Julie Ann: Because they are actually doing the work.

Larry: Yes, they are doing the work! Why wouldn't you want their opinion? I have an old saying in my old business, people would ask, what kind of trucks do you buy? And I'd say, I buy the trucks the drivers tell me they like the best. And they would say . . .

Julie Ann: What?

Larry: Yes. I'd tell them I don't drive the truck and I don't do the driving. I'm going to talk to the guy doing the job to find out what the tool needs to be, and that makes sense. And to your point, when you involve people, ask their opinions, it elevates them in so many ways, and it makes them a better, more involved, and a more integral part of your business. They feel like they are part of you, not working for you, and it makes for a more productive employee.

Julie Ann: Absolutely, and a more loyal employee.

Larry: No doubt.

Julie Ann: With the workforce shrinking, as it is, it becomes more and more important for people to feel like they are a part of the company, not just a number or somebody who is doing a little piece. Your little piece makes a difference.

Larry: No question. Absolutely. And amazingly, the very, very best ideas always come from the field, always. They don't come from the boardroom, they just don't.

Julie Ann: I think that is a lesson that can be learned by a lot of leaders out there because that happens way too often. I'm going to give you an example, and I won't name the company. Because I have been around business so much, it just cracked me up. So, I use a certain powder when I am feeling sick to make me feel better, and it's not illegal. It comes in a jar because you are supposed to use a tablespoon, and you can put the tablespoon in the jar. They called me on the phone and told me, one of your orders will be in glass. I'm thinking, plastic jar, glass jar, who cares? What did they do? They put the powder in a pill bottle! Not only can't you get a tablespoon in, you can't get a teaspoon in!

Larry: My first thought was how do you get it out?

Julie Ann: So, I called them, and I asked who thought of this? Obviously it was no one who had ever used the product. Do you know how much powder I would waste, which isn't cheap, trying to tap, tap, tap the powder onto a spoon?

Larry: Right.

Julie Ann: It was the most amazing thing to me because I couldn't believe anybody actually did this. Whoever thought this was a great idea because they ran out of the jars for a while, never used the product, or didn't read the label.

Larry: Great analogy. They never used it themselves.

Julie Ann: It's kind of like you saying to your drivers, I'm going to put you into this little, teeny car that you can't even put a tire in the back of.

Larry: Exactly. Let's tie your hands up and get you to do the job.

Julie Ann: So, good for you! Kudos to you! Maybe you already realize, and leaders are doing it more and more; being open to the people who are actually on the phones, doing the customer service, doing the work behind the product are the ones who have the best information.

Larry: I agree. I think there are a lot of people, who give it lip service, but don't believe it, and I think that's where the rubber meets the road. You have to mean it, and you have to really want to hear it and not just placate for the purpose of making them feel better. That's the difference. It's got to be real. And when it is real, they know it. Anybody in the company, drivers, phone people, anyone, knows if they have an idea, they can call me, they can text me, they can email me. They all have my cell phone. I'll ask the drivers, what do you think of this? They are not intimidated by who I am. And I don't want them to be intimidated by who I am.

Julie Ann: And you probably get a lot more great ideas than somebody who is standoffish. Or people who don't feel they can go in that office.

Larry: Exactly.

Julie Ann: I'm reading through a couple of more employee engagement ideas you have. I love these because you are getting down to the root of the people. Outsiders might think you would normally have a lot of turnover, but I'm guessing for you that's not a big problem.

Larry: It is not. We have a ton of folks who have been here for a very, very long time.

A perfect example is I am thinking of a store right up the road from me in Ocala, where there is a staff of 12 people, and I promise you that seven of those have been there for more than 12 years. And the others have only been added because the store needed more folks. The base staff is the same staff, and it is one of the most successful stores in the country because of that retention, and the way they work together. Like anyone else, as we grow, we need more people. Hiring and recruiting and looking for new people is what we do, but turnover has not been one of our biggest issues. We have it, because it happens, but it is not one of our biggest issues.

Julie Ann: I love this quote by you. Maybe you will tell me that you didn't say it, yet after talking to you for a while, it sounds like you. It says, "Somebody once told you that if you ever want to be a success, just hire people who are smarter than you." And you said, "Ma'am, that's going to be easy. I'm from Oklahoma."

Larry: I did say that. While it may seem apropos it really is true. Some of these clichés you hear of all your life and I've thought, given where I am from, given my education, given my upbringing, my level of success is improbable it doesn't make sense. I did not finish college. I had an abusive father and was raised in a single-mom household. All of these things that are supposed to be strikes against you. I just think that the statement of, "hire people smarter than you," is very simple, but so true. Get people around you that are good at what they do. Then to really be a great leader is to shut up and listen. You really don't have to do any more than that. It's absolutely amazing and I am dumbfounded sometimes. People say look at what you have accomplished, and I'm like, yeah, okay.

Julie Ann: And I think that's why people say you are a very humble person. I think it comes from you accepting that you don't know everything. Too many times people who are a president of a company don't understand that they don't have all the answers. And sometimes it's not even their fault. It's the pressure that they have allowed upon themselves. When I coach CEOs and people in the C-suite, they allow the pressure they are under to make them feel like they have to have all the answers. And when I can say to them, you know what, you don't. You may even become a better leader if you reveal you don't. This has become a hot topic now, that good leaders should be a little more vulnerable; they are just starting to discover that maybe it is okay. And you have been doing it all along! So, you are ahead of the curve!

Larry: In my case, I didn't have a choice! (Laughing). I really didn't have the answers!

Julie Ann: Little did you know you were a trendsetter.

Larry: That's right. Exactly. When my leaders come to me, and they do, and ask me what I think about a problem, I try to hold them accountable. I tell them if they bring me a problem, to bring me three solutions. Then, we can talk about which one of the solutions is the best. And often, when they just bring me a problem with no solutions, I actually send them out, and say I can give that some thought, but I think you can probably come up with some solutions. So, why don't you come up with some solutions, then come back and see me. You know what happens 90 percent of the time? They come up with the perfect solution on their own. It's not that I really don't have the answer . . .

Julie Ann: You want them to grow.

Larry: It is better if they come up with it themselves and not rely on someone else every time there is an issue.

Julie Ann: That is so amazing because I was just working with a leadership team yesterday, and that was one of their complaints. People are always bothering them with problems, and that was my suggestion.

Larry: That is great.

Julie Ann: If they come to them with a problem, ask them to come up with a solution if they haven't already. Sometimes once you ask them to do that, they may never come back to you again. The chronic complainers will not come back because they don't want to hear that. And the ones who can work it through will not need to come to you right away. They will find out and will grow themselves and realize they can come up with a solution. Or, they come up with a solution and realize that in the bigger picture, it's not going to work.

Larry: And a lot of times, you can let them try something that you already know is not going to work because guess what they will learn?

Julie Ann: It's not going to work. They learn by doing, as long as it's not going to hurt the company.

Larry: Right. No long-term damage, it may cost a little money, but...

Julie Ann: But it costs less

Larry and Julie Ann (together): In the long run.

Larry: My absolute, 1,000-percent belief is that the mistakes are some of the most valuable experiences you will have in your lifetime, if you choose to allow them to be valuable experiences. We talk about that with our folks, all the time. We don't admonish people who make mistakes, we ask them what they have learned, and if they learned the right thing, we say a congratulation, that's great. You won.

Julie Ann: Well, kudos to you again. I think you are an exceptional leader. I've talked to a lot of leaders, so I think I can say that. While we are talking about congratulations, we have a few minutes left. And everybody has a way to monetarily give gifts to their employees. I would like you to talk about what you do that's a little different.

Larry: You know, obviously we have the standard things that everyone does. We have the savings, the insurance, all of the benefits, and so forth and so on. What I am a firm believer in with additional monetary rewards, is to establish some goals. Let people establish where they are going to be, and then give them phenomenal awards. A perfect example of that this past year is that we wanted to see some significant growth in all of our core stores that we own. Not franchise stores, but stores that we actually own. I went to every manager and asked them to give me a stretch on each store, if everything was perfect, and they did everything right. We asked them, where could they be at the end of the year, on December 15? So, each one turned in where they thought they could be. We called it their stretch goal. We came back and said, here is what we are going to do. We are going to make it the best Christmas your families have ever had. They are already on a great compensation package, no question about it, and they already get bonuses. I said if you hit your stretch goal, I'm going to personally deliver you $10,000 in cash for Christmas on December 15, so that your family can have the best Christmas they have ever had. And so we set that in motion in all 15 stores, and this past December, on December 15, I actually visited nine stores, and handed out $110,000 in cash bonuses. (Some reached their goals early so they created a double stretch and got additional monies.) It was like you just gave someone 10 million dollars.

Julie Ann: And you let them figure out what that stretch was.

Larry: Absolutely.

Julie Ann: It was not something you put on them.

Larry: Yeah. And this was above and beyond any other compensation. We called it a stretch bonus. It was the best Christmas ever. We will do things like that all the time. I call them, "Found Money" programs.

Julie Ann: I want to get in on that.

Larry: Every year, we have something pretty exciting like that going on. I used to do it with my old company too. We'd give away motorcycles, cars, and things like that. We'd just make it fun. We have an annual picnic and the tire company comes over to Busch Gardens for a family day. We take them for about an hour and forty-five minutes in the middle of the day, and we give out about $50,000 cash to employees. And everybody gets something. It's really amazing, and people feel like they are a part of something that is fun and growing. It is great to see that kind of thing with families. We are very family-oriented. We like things that are implemented to make their lives better.

It's not just employees, but it's about families, leaders, and everyone across the board.

Julie Ann: You have got it together. You may be from Oklahoma, but you have it together. And if someone is listening from Oklahoma, I'm just kidding because he is the one who brought it up; it wasn't me.

Larry: We joke about it. And everybody from Oklahoma jokes about it.

Julie Ann:	I have a feeling that you and I could probably talk for several hours, but unfortunately, we are running out of time.
Larry:	You are right, and I am enjoying it myself.
Julie Ann:	You've had some profound thoughts and great ideas, but if you had to give out one step, one idea that the listener could take with them right now, into their company to start being the best leader they could be, which one would you choose?
Larry:	I would say focus on serving, not service. The reason I say that is that we find by serving your employees, as opposed to over lording them, that they will serve their customers in the very same manner. So, we look at our hierarchy as an upside-down pyramid. I work for everybody in the company, not the other way around. I would say start from you being at the bottom of the pyramid, not the top, and serve everyone above you. And then you will see everyone above you do the same thing and you will get results.

Favorite Food – Southern Fried Chicken

Shut up and listen…if it were only that easy. Creating a culture where people are engaged, loyal and productive, takes more than just listening, but it is a great place to start. Listening gives you the ability to be open to new ideas and catapult your business to new heights. Listening helps you identify what people in your company want and need. They are after all, as Larry says, the people you serve before your customers even interact. You have two ears and one mouth for a reason. The next time you are in a conversation with your workforce, listen more and talk less. I think the results will surprise you.

HOW TO BUILD RELATIONSHIPS WITHIN YOUR WORKFORCE

WITH STEVE BROWNE, VP OF HR, LaROSA'S PIZZA

"Get the mission statement and the vision statement off the walls and into hearts."

Steve Browne

STEVE BROWN IS THE VICE PRESIDENT and Director of Human Resources (HR) for LaRosa's Inc, which is a regional pizzeria restaurant chain in the Midwest. He's been in HR for 30 plus years. He's also the author of HR On Purpose. He has his own blog called, Everyday People, and now he serves on the board of SHRM, The Society of Human Resource Management.

I first met Steve when I was invited to be a part of the National SHRM Blog Squad in Chicago. You would never guess Steve was an executive. Steve is the guy in the trenches, with an open ear and an open heart. His style of activating the employee experience is to be with the people he is serving, literally. After doing this interview, I imagined working with Steve would be a lot like going into business with your high school best friend. And Steve knows very intimately about having fun, as he travels around the country speaking about HR, he has a suitcase full of toys that travel with him to explain his style of leadership. Yes, I said toys. Each has its own meaning and memory. This type of authenticity allows those that work with Steve to be who they are. His style and dedication to creating a great place to work was a perfect match for Businesses that Care.

CONVERSATION WITH JULIE ANN AND STEVE:

Julie Ann: Steve, thanks for joining us.

Steve: Hi, Julie Ann. Thanks for having me.

Julie Ann: How long have you been at LaRosa's?

Steve: I've been here 12 years this year.

Julie Ann: That shows something right there. You must like the culture. When you came in, did you have culture shock? Were things not as great as you would have liked them, or did you kind of step into paradise? How'd that work?

Steve: When I came here, HR was called the black hole.

Julie Ann: Not a good frame of reference there.

Steve: Not at all. The person who was here before me did a great job, because she put a lot of structure into the company and compliance-oriented HR. However, it wasn't very connected to our pizzerias, which is where our business hums. Those are the people that do the best work in our company, so I wanted to turn it around and make it more human centric and they've allowed me to do that.

Julie Ann: It's all about relationships. I'm a huge relationship person. That's one reason I do this podcast. I was just discussing with a client this morning about the importance of what the millennials have brought to the workplace regarding how important relationships are. Good on them for doing that, because it was missing. Before nobody was stepping up and saying, "We need to have real relationships if you want me to work harder and smarter and be a good problem solver for you."

Steve: Absolutely. I agree.

Julie Ann: So how are you doing that?

Steve: Treating people genuinely. Meeting them where they are at. Not coming in as some pretentious HR group or corporate staff. We go and meet them for who they are. We hire 16-year olds, but we also have people in their 80s working right next to them. So we try to treat them all as team members. We don't use it as a catch phrase. We don't have a bunch of posters that say, "You're on the team." It's much more, "Hi, Julie Ann. I'm Steve." As an example, I don't wear any LaRosa's logo wear when I go into the restaurants. I just walk in and go straight into the kitchen to see if anybody will catch me. And then when they don't, they'll say, "Who is this guy and what's he doing and why is he walking around?" I say, "Oh, hi, what do you do?" And then, I introduce myself as Steve. Not Steve from HR or Steve from corporate.

Julie Ann: Do they ever call the police on you?

Steve: I've had a few people tell the manager, "There's a guy in the back." And the manager says, "Oh, that's Steve, he's cool." The whole point is trying to take away the obstacles and the barriers and the preconceptions so they know they have someone they can talk to. My boss made sure part of my job description was that I am the safe haven of the company.

Steve: Which is huge, so, anybody can talk to me about anything, literally. Having some of those baselines, Julie Ann, really helps us establish the culture in a more people-oriented way, more often. We still struggle, but we do pretty well.

Julie Ann: Everyone is going to have struggles. Everyone is going to falter. I consider myself a communications specialist and no matter what kind of work I'm doing with a company, whether it's coaching their leadership or helping them create a better culture or engaging strategic leadership. It all comes down to communication and how people talk to one another. Sometimes it's the words you use, for instance, you don't say, "I'm Steve. I'm the Director, the VP Director of HR." That's not how you start a conversation. You start a conversation with, "I'm Steve." In other words, I'm a person and you're a person.

Steve: Exactly.

I think it's worked a lot better, because we're much better at knowing each other by name. We don't put as much credibility as we should in knowing each other's names. We give kids name tags for a reason, you know? We want them to know each other by name so there's a personal side to who we are. We're a family pizzeria, that's in our brand. So, you need to have things be a little more accessible and names are the easiest way to start that out.

Julie Ann: That's so true. That's why whatever networking event you go to, whatever conference you go to, everybody has a name tag for a reason. They only need to figure out a way to make them so they'll fit on your shoulder, instead of down by your navel. I'm just saying.

Steve: I agree.

Julie Ann: Another important part of what you said is listening, because people always think communication is speaking and it's so much more about listening. As I was making an online class video yesterday and I said, "We have two ears and one mouth. There had to be a reason for that."

Steve: Absolutely.

Julie Ann: Great idea of you being a safe haven and having it known. In other words, communicating that to people, that you're a safe haven, instead of assuming that people know that.

Steve: Yes, and I don't get upset. I don't get embarrassed. I don't judge. I'll listen to anything. I could tell you stories that would curl your hair, but that's not the point. They need to know that they can talk about what's going on in their lives. I think as HR people, as business people, we tell everybody, "Bring 100% to work," or "110% to work," all these motivational things. But don't bring your life, because that's awful. My thing is everybody brings their life, it's inevitable. You need to let them do that, because once they're more connected and can share who they are genuinely at work, they'll do their work better. They'll know they're listened to, and honestly, they'll perform, because they want to. They really do.

Julie Ann: And they're going to bring their life anyway.

Steve: Right, no doubt.

Julie Ann: You could tell them to leave it at home, but they're not going to. They feel freer to be who they are and be vulnerable. The idea of vulnerability is becoming something that is preferred in leadership. People want leaders who are vulnerable and authentic and are able to say, "Oh, I was in a bad mood yesterday. I'm sorry." That's who people want to work for and that's who I want to work for.

Steve: Absolutely. I agree.

Julie Ann: When you came and you started this, you were really changing the dynamic that was going on between corporate and your stores. Did you find some resistance from people? How did you overcome that?

Steve: The way I overcame it was, I have the best boss I've ever had in my career here. To your point earlier of listening, he told me in my first three months that I'm supposed to listen. No programs. No ideas. No implementation, just find out. Get the lay of the land. The person who was before me led HR from her desk. I lead from the stores. I'm in the stores and they say, "It's HR," and I say, "Oh, hey, this is scary," and I just play around. Appropriately, but you know, treat them like people. It just took time and consistency and visibility and being genuine. I come in and I'll make jokes and I'll let them laugh and I want to hear their stories. The more I got to know them as people and kept doing it with my behavior, not preaching it, but living it, walls started coming down. Also, when I did hit resistance and obstacles, I confronted it and I said, "Okay, this is how it was. I understand that. But this is how we're going to do it now. Are you with me? Does this make sense for you? Can you perform to this? Yes or no? And if you can't, how can we get you to perform to it?" It's an ongoing process. I tend to look at HR more along a continuum, than I do start and stop, because I'm dealing with people differently every day, with their situations, which are different every day, and I love that. They were used to rules, regulations, policies, procedures, and disciplines.

Julie Ann: With no gray areas.

Steve: Oh, it was black and that was it. It wasn't black or white. It was one. Now it's gray and beautiful.

Julie Ann: Well, I think that's true authenticity and I love your idea of consistency and visibility. I like that, because you have to have consistency for anything to grow within a company. You've been there 12 years now, but for any C-suite executive out there that's just coming into a company. I think your boss was right on when he said no changes for three months. That's what people fear the most when someone new comes into the C-suite.

Steve: Right.

Julie Ann: Three months of this new behavior of your visibility is so important to get people to change their behavior. That consistency shows you're walking your talk.

Steve: I try to tell people, get the mission statement and the vision statement off the walls and into hearts, because when people see it on your sleeve, they'll do anything for you. But they also need to know that you'll do anything for them, it can't be one sided, it has to be reciprocated. I have team members that don't have a high education or come from different economic backgrounds or race, gender, and age, all of the diversity categories. However, it's Julie Ann, Bob, Susie, and David. It's not a label; it's a person who happens to have all these wonderful qualities about them. We're taking the chance to start teaching people this more ongoing, so it's not just me. I want to develop my store managers to do this with their team and then their team members. I'm very excited about having the chance to do that. It should be fun.

Julie Ann: Kind of building it into the normal everyday process of what you do.

Steve: I want it to be the fabric. I don't want it to be the program. I want it to be the fabric.

Julie Ann: That's funny, because I use that all the time about building tools and skills into the fabric of a business, because then it's like breathing. It's not something you think about anymore. That's just the way it is, this is the culture. This is the atmosphere. This is our workforce. This is what we do. When that's really strong in a company, it's really easy to rid yourself of people who don't align with that. They see it everywhere and if, for instance, somebody comes in and they just have a really strong, judgmental personality, it's going to be really uncomfortable for them to be at LaRosa's and that's just fine. Right?

Steve: I agree.

Julie Ann: They kind of self-disappear, as opposed to you moving them out, which is a lot more difficult.

Steve: Very true.

Julie Ann: Some of the businesses that I've interviewed have used this podcast for recruiting. Wherever they have their jobs, they have them listen to the podcast and then, they use that as part of their interview process.

Steve: Nice.

Julie Ann: People get to hear this is what our culture is like and some people say, "Wow, I want to work there." I had a client tell me they were having a really hard time filling a position. They had put our podcast on their website, where their job availability was, when they asked the candidate what made her come in, she said it was the podcast, because that's the community I want to be with.

Steve: Oh, cool.

Julie Ann: Or you might have people say, "I don't like that."

Steve: And then they need to go away.

Julie Ann: That saves everybody a lot of time and money. You're building a culture and by having it resonate in everything you do, everybody knows what it is. You probably change many lives for the better, because when people learn to become less judgmental, they get along with the rest of the world a lot better. If you go into the world only looking for people just like you, you're going to be pretty lonely and pretty irritated.

Steve: Absolutely.

Julie Ann: We've got to learn to love what people have to offer, no matter how different they are than ourselves.

Steve: Correct.

Julie Ann: I had read about something that you do that's a little different when people have a work anniversary. You don't just send them a certificate in the mail. Talk to us about what you do. It's unique and I think it's a really good practice.

Steve: We used to do traditional things, like most companies. We had a banquet and we brought everybody in and we didn't consider the person who was actually the one to be focused on or celebrate. We would have these banquets with people we didn't know and who worked part time and shift work and this big feast and it was awful. The CEO and my boss, the COO, said, "Hey, I don't care what we do, just change it." And I said, "Well, what is my budget?" And they said, "Make it work, we'll figure it out," And I went, "Okay." What I came up with was I would go see you where you were working at the time. I would bring people that work with you, in operations or in the call center or in the corporate office or in the bakery, to wherever you are, I would bring your supervisors together and we would talk about you and thank you for five, 10, 15, 20 minutes. I would bring a bag of cookies and a gift card and balloons. When you get 10 years, we bring a tray for the whole location and it feeds 50 people. What has really changed is people start saying, "Is the cookie guy coming? It's my anniversary. He's late. Where is he at?" We just had a server that we celebrated for serving tables for 15 years.

Julie Ann: Wow.

Steve: And when I came into the restaurant and pulled her aside, she came out and hugged the cookie tray. She's like, "I got them. This is the best thing ever!" I've had people cry and hug and say, "You thought of me. I didn't even know you knew I existed." I'm trying to show, again, model the behavior I expect in others. I will tell my wife, "Hey, Sunday night I'm going to go to our Boudinot restaurant, which is an hour away, because Mary is having her 10th anniversary and I need to be there." My wife's reaction, "Absolutely." So now that we do it where people are, it makes them less embarrassed and less put off. We get to know who they are as a person. To me, it's genuine recognition and it's cookies and balloons. It's so simple, but those five, 10 minutes with them, buys me another three years. I mean, honestly it really does.

Julie Ann: How big is your territory? From where you are in corporate office, how many miles is it around you?

Steve: Probably 50 miles. We have 13 locations. The farthest store away from me, from the office, is about an hour and a half. We're pretty regional. If I'm at home when we're open, I go. I want to value what they do, because if I don't value you for who you are and what you do, it's not really recognition in my book.

Julie Ann: I know and I love that you go on their shift, whatever that shift is. You don't make them come in the middle of the day if they don't work in the middle of the day. You're really serving them, as opposed to, "We'll celebrate you when it's convenient for me."

Steve: It has really changed the executives in the C-suite, because they say, "Well, Julie Ann only works Saturday at 5:00?" I said, "Yes, what are you going to do? I'm going to meet her Saturday at 5:00 and I want you to be there." The coolest thing happened, oh, gosh, a month ago? I went out to see a delivery driver on her 20th year anniversary; on a Friday night and Friday nights are by far our busiest night. Our CEO had another obligation. He called me on the way there, and says, "Have you seen her yet?" And I said, "No." He says, "When you get there, give me the phone." I said, "Okay." So, I got there and I said, "Hey, we're here to celebrate. By the way, here's a phone call." And the CEO said, "I'm so sorry I couldn't be there. I love everything you do. Thank you for being with us for 20 years. You make our company phenomenal and I wish I could see you. The next time I get a chance, I'll come out and see you." It was fantastic.

Julie Ann: And did he go see her?

Steve: He has, yes.

Julie Ann: How meaningful. First of all, it's phenomenal you had a driver for 20 years. Let's be real.

Steve: That's normal here.

Julie Ann: I know, but that says something about your company right away, because who would think that a driver would be with you for 20 years? You have to be doing something right for someone to do that. I'm sure we could go to 100 other pizza places where drivers, if they're lucky, stay there for two weeks, right?

Steve: Correct.

Julie Ann: What your company has done is you appreciate every day they're there. You get them to stay longer because you are appreciating them instead of assuming they're going to screw you somewhere along the line by leaving after a short period of time

Steve: Right. The other thing we've seen, which we didn't anticipate, I absolutely didn't anticipate. Is when we do a celebration for a person, all of the team members that are there witness it. Then they'll say, "When do I get my cookies? Are you coming back?" I answered, "Well, how many years have you been here?" So, we have all of these really meaningful conversations and it allows them to see themselves at the company, which is priceless to me.

Julie Ann: That epitomizes my slogan of, simple solutions for big results. You're talking cookies and balloons. You're not buying everybody a car.

Steve: They're amazing cookies.

Julie Ann: But it's really that you're delivering them, right? I mean that's really the bottom line of what they're really appreciating. For many people, working for a pizzeria, in their own judgmental mind, they probably never figured anybody would really care one way or the other. Then, that probably gets you more good employees, because people working for you are telling other people how good you treat your employees.

Steve:	Right. And back to the story of, I don't tell them my title or where I'm from, when I come in with the cookies, they say, "Oh, there's Steve." They don't say, "Oh, there's the executive of HR. Oh my gosh." It's, "Hey, it's the guy with the cookies. What's up, Steve?" I'm trying to teach the people in the office, this is how you want to be seen. You know, not as a peer, but as a...I don't know what the right word is, a fellow human.
Julie Ann:	Yes. A colleague, right?
Steve:	Yes, a colleague. Right.
Julie Ann:	One of the episodes I do with internal podcasting is with the CEO and maybe some other people in the C-suite. I ask them not about their job or how they got there or where they went to school or what's their experience. Instead, I ask them, "What's your favorite movie?"
Steve:	Oh, excellent.
Julie Ann:	"Why? What kind of music do you like to listen to? If you could go anywhere in the world, where would it be? Why?" And then, when that goes out to the inner workings of the company and the workforce listens to it, they're connected now. Just like what you're saying about you're Steve or the cookie guy. Not the HR VP. The internal podcast creates the same relationship. Now it's not the CEO, it's, "Oh, that's Bob." The next time they see them somewhere, they still feel connected. "Wow, he likes The Grateful Dead. I love The Grateful Dead." That humanizes the people in the corporate office. Do you have any other ideas that you've come up with that our listeners can use? That's the whole point of the podcast is for the listeners to say, "Why didn't we think of that? That's easy. Let's do that."

Steve: The other thing I teach people is to stop being firefighters at work, stop thinking that everything is a fire. Something very simple to remember, is whatever situation they face that leads to frustration or conflict or confrontation, simply step back and breathe. Get your thoughts together and then reassess and address things. When I first started, our personnel files were like two to three inches thick with discipline. Now they're less than a quarter of an inch because we're generating conversation and feedback. We needed to teach them how to calm down and not overreact. It seems simple, but people just overlook it all the time.

Julie Ann: That's really funny. Another way you and I are alike, because when I teach communication, the word I use is pause. People need to learn how to pause. You remember, when you were a kid, you heard, "Count to 10 before you speak," if you're mad. That's a really good idea to take into adulthood.

Steve: Yes, and I think it helps them understand their culture, because every one of us gets frustrated. Everyone. Instead of avoiding it or giving them some big program, just say, "I know you're struggling. Here's a tool. Try this. Move this way." Shape their behavior and have them look more broadly, instead of focusing on the difficulty in front of them.

Julie Ann: Okay. Well, you and I could spend another half hour on perspective, because that's a big word for me too, but we don't have time for that, but maybe another time. Thank you so much for being on Businesses That Care.

Steve: Thanks. I really appreciate it. It's been fun to talk to you. I can't wait to see you and meet you at SHRM. It'll be fun. (And it was)

Favorite Food: Pizza...(Big surprise)

Balloons and cookies, is that all it takes? No, but if you add generosity of yourself, that's a great recipe. When was the last time you experienced leadership as one of the team members? The mistake that is made is leadership sometimes thinks they have to abandon authority for authenticity or vulnerability.

When rules and boundaries are created to move everyone towards success AND the workforce knows why and how that will be accomplished, authority is not lost. It is respected when there is a process for expressing the why and the how of your company's vision. Basically, you are ridding your organization of the theory that people need to do as you say, but not as you do. You are replacing it with a culture built on ideas and ideals that are supported and followed by everyone for a common goal. Can you create that in your workplace? Absolutely.

BUILD A BUSINESS LIKE A LIVING ORGANISM

WITH SHERYL O'LOUGHLIN, CEO, REBBL

We have to change the way we think, in order to have a different outcome...Hopefully we will start with a new approach to business as biology, instead of business as a machine.

Sheryl O'Loughlin

WHILE INTERVIEWING KEVIN McCARTHY for my podcast, he suggested he might have a good guest for me. Shuffling through papers he mentioned her name was Sheryl O'Loughlin, but he wasn't sure of the company name. Then he said, here it is and started to spell it. R E B...before he got another letter out, I screamed, Rebbl? OMG, their new drinks were my new addiction. At that moment I didn't even care if they had a good culture. As it turns out, to create that great product, you also have to have a great team. That team flourishes in a great culture.

In Forbes magazine it says that Sheryl O'Loughlin, the former CEO of Clif Bar® is trying to get America to drink herbs. Sheryl is a serial success story who has worked at Kraft®, Quaker Oats®, and doubled revenue at Clif Bar®. She created a company called Plum Organics® and sold it to Campbell's®. You can't have that kind of success without knowing how to treat a workforce as your partner. Sheryl has creative ways to build a culture that delivers success within and outside the company. This interview is an education in having a successful business, a healthier life and a more compassionate world.

Conversation with Julie Ann and Sheryl:

Julie Ann: Thank you Sheryl, so much for making time today to be with us.

Sheryl: It is such an honor to be here. Thank you. I already have enjoyed our conversation prior to getting on air. So, I am very excited.

Julie Ann: Yeah, we are like twin sisters from different mothers. It is fantastic. First, why don't you tell people about Rebbl, which I have six of in my refrigerator right now. I don't really think I have ever interviewed anyone where I have used their product and was so excited about it. I found Rebbl a couple of months ago at a Whole Foods store in the refrigerator by the checkout. The word chocolate caught my eye, as it will do, and I got chocolate and I got mocha, and the rest is history. Tell us about these drinks, the back story and the incredible person who is putting this product together.

Sheryl: I tell you I feel the same way about being part of this company. When I left Plum, actually when I left Stanford, I had been running the Center for Entrepreneurial studies at Stanford, then Plum sold, and we moved to wine country. I thought to myself, I'm just going to be on boards, and I'm going to teach entrepreneurship and ride into the sunset. Then Palo, he is our Chief Innovation Officer, and the most brilliant beverage innovator I've met in my entire life, asked me to be on the board, which led to, can you help us through this fundraising. I said okay, I'll do it for a little while; I'll be the interim CEO.

The more I learned about this company, the more I was blown away because it had the magic that I had seen in these other great brands.

Julie Ann: Do you think that was his plan all along?

Sheryl: Yeah. He was in the CEO job, and he didn't want it. He hated it. He was like somebody take this from me! But it is just a special experience in so many ways. I can't even begin to tell you! It starts with what you were talking about, the product itself. It is an organic, coconut milk-based beverage that contains herbs, some known as adaptogens, one being Ashwagandha. Ashwagandha has been shown through clinical studies to actually help your body regulate stress. So if you are highly-stressed it will calm you down. If you are under-stressed it will lift you up and give you energy.

Julie Ann: That's what it does for me.

Sheryl: That's what you said with the mushrooms, the Reishi mushrooms. The stuff works! People are discovering what we have known, in ancient wisdom, forever. This stuff really works. It's a natural, true functional drink. The best part is that Palo is just a beautiful craftsman, a true artist. This is his art, and he wants it to taste exquisite. It is amazing to me after all the experiences I've had, many people don't understand that at the end of the day, it's food it's a beverage. It could be very organic, and very healthy, but until it is something that is truly enjoyable for people, then you are not getting the full experience of what the beverage is all about, and what it can do for your life. It is something to enjoy and savor, versus something just to force your way through.

Julie Ann:	I was telling Sheryl before we started that I start my mornings with hot water and lemon. And then some mornings, I'll have a Rebbl drink. That lasts me until lunchtime. I haven't any problem going to lunchtime.
Sheryl:	It fills you up, it truly satisfies you, and it's a very nourishing, dense drink.
Julie Ann:	And it tastes delicious!
Sheryl:	And you said you actually drink it for dessert sometimes with your Whole Foods salad.
Julie Ann:	That's right. I travel a lot. Instead of going out to dinner at a restaurant and sitting in some corner by myself, which is just a horrible vision (I don't do that), I'll find a Whole Foods if I can. And I will go to their salad bar and grab a Rebbl. That's my dessert and my drink and I'm as happy as can be.
Sheryl:	This makes me so happy. Thank you, even though you are buying out all the shelves in Pittsburgh.
Julie Ann:	That's the way it goes. You snooze you lose, right? They can order cases just like me.
Sheryl:	There you go, with a discount.
Julie Ann:	So tell me a little bit about what goes on inside the company that you are running, and what's different about your culture, your employee engagement, and your employee experience.
Sheryl:	Well, I have to begin by starting at the beginning of the company. Because how the company began and the purpose behind it, that in and of itself, drives almost everything we do. So this company was actually created out of a non-profit called Not For Sale.
Julie Ann:	I like that name.

Sheryl: Yeah, it's ironic. People don't understand what we mean when we talk about it. It was started through the effort of Dave Batstone, who is the founder of Not For Sale. His whole goal with the organization was to create a future without human trafficking. Human Trafficking is the fastest growing illegal industry in the world. It's in the top three and is right up there with the drug trade and the illegal weapons trade. It happens right here in this country. I'm in California right now, in Oakland, and it's happening right now.

Julie Ann: It happens here, too. I am very close with a woman here who is very big on educating people about trafficking and working with people like the trucking industry to be on the lookout because a lot of it happens on the road in weird places.

Sheryl: Not only that, but slave labor affects my industry and is partly why we were created. It is something that people are impacted by all over the world. It is in greater numbers than we ever expected, the sex trade and slave trade. So what happened was Dave Batstone pulled together the greatest thinkers that he knew in a group to address the slave trade issue that was happening in Peru at the time. He pulled together an agronomist, a major-league baseball player, Jeremy Affeldt, who used to play for the Giants. He pulled together venture capitalists and he created this unique meeting and he called it the Montara Circle. Then, he boldly put them into groups, not knowing what would come out of this session, and committed to funding the best idea that came out to address this trafficking issue.

Julie Ann: Kind of like his own Shark Tank.

Sheryl: Totally, and that was really bold because he had no idea what was going to come out. It could have been the crappiest ideas in the world. One team, which included the baseball player and the agronomist talked, about using the herbs from this community in Peru in a drink. At the time they called it a smart tea. So, this idea would be that we buy the herbs, we help the livelihood of the indigenous people there, so they are not susceptible to middlemen coming in and buying their crops for nothing.

Julie Ann: I've got to interrupt you and ask you what's an agronomist?

Sheryl: Agronomists work on the land, basically. So they are looking at crops and the different ways you use crops. So, it was the perfect person for this kind of session. It morphed, when a year later, they hired, Palo Hawken. This guy is the chief innovation officer, the creator of our products that I was referring to. They brought him in, and what he eventually created is what we now see on the shelves as Rebbl. The idea behind it is we give two-and-a-half percent of our net sales, not profits, to Not For Sale, the non-profit I mentioned before. Regardless if we make profits, this two-and-a-half percent of net sales supports their work on rehabilitating people who have been trafficked in areas such as: education, housing, health care and training.

Julie Ann: Mental health services.

Sheryl: That's just down the river, right? We have to address the issue up the river. Since we buy ingredients from over 26 countries, everywhere we go we focus very much on the livelihood of the grower. Whether it is through making sure they make a living wage, to health care, to making sure they have access to education. Because we know that in these communities, if they are thriving, they are not going to be vulnerable to trafficking. So, we address the issues in two ways, that and the people coming to work at Rebbl, knowing every day they are fighting human trafficking, man, there is nothing more motivating than that! That was a long-winded answer to your question because everything we do in the company, we do to reinforce that purpose at the end of the day.

Julie Ann: How do you do that? How do you let them know on a constant basis that's what it's all about? Because a lot of times in companies I find they have a great idea, or they have a great cause, or they have a great mission statement, or they have great values, but, you know, they give it to you in your on-boarding process and that's the end of it. So what do you do that other companies could use to make sure that this idea, this giving-back is a constant thought in their work?

Sheryl: Gosh, there are numerous ways. Just when you start, at the very basic, I obsessively talk about it. I was just talking to one of my investors, whom I adore, about some of the work we are doing around what we call impact. How do we positively impact peoples' lives? I was having a conversation with the group that is specifically focused on projects involving impact, even though the whole company is involved, since they are on the forefront of it. We were talking about our environmental efforts and our humanitarian efforts, and the manager of the program was saying to me, how do we think about all of these different priorities? There are so many. There are so many things we can do? I said to her that we always have to look at it from our lens of what our essence is, the essence of our company. It came out of the birth of our company.

It is seeing the world without human trafficking. So, everything we think about, in terms of our priorities, whether they are environmental or humanitarian, need to come through that lens. Let me give you a very specific example, climate change. We are part of an initiative called the Climate Collaborative in the natural food world, and we are taking a leadership role in it, to address climate change. The natural food industry should be at the forefront of that, and we have been very behind. We wanted to be part of this movement and make it an essential part of what we do. So, you may ask what does that have to do with trafficking? What I remind the company of, through constant communication, is if these communities are impacted by climate change, and there are droughts, for example, they cannot plant their crops. Their livelihood is diminished, and that makes them vulnerable to trafficking. So everything connects back into the core. Let me give you an example from the other end of the spectrum, programs we do within our company to support peoples' wellness. If we stand for, what is essentially, equality and inclusion because if you have equality and inclusion, you wouldn't have these issues with trafficking in our world. We need to look within and make sure we are taking care of our own people. We were thinking about parental leave and putting a program in place to support that. We figured out we can't just give it to the primary caregiver, but rather it must also be to the secondary caregivers, so both people have the opportunity to stay home with this gift of their child. In addition, we need to support people who are going through adoption, not just natural childbirth. It's a simple example, but we put everything through this lens. When people start getting in the practice of putting it through the lens, they start to realize that this is such an ecosystem. A business is a living system, and everything we do impacts everything else. So if we understand the total . . .

Julie Ann: Oh, gosh! I've got to stop you right there! If every company really internalized that everything they do affects every person and place around them, we'd live in a different world. There would be more success in businesses, and there would be fewer turnovers. That one idea of, everything we do affects everything we do; everything inside affects everything outside.

Sheryl: Well, it's funny you bring it up. We don't have to diverge down this path very far, but I am part of this group, the community group, that is called the Regenerative Business. One woman who is leading this movement is Carol Sanders. What the movement is about is regenerative agriculture which you are going to hear more and more about. Let me give you a simple example that goes to the essence of the ecosystem. A lot of our soil is not healthy anymore because we haven't created an ecosystem that supports it. From growing organically, the animals that are part of the system, to the bio-diversity that we have there, how healthy are the people that are able to take care of the crop? There's an ecosystem there. So, taking that same model of a living system and then putting it in on a business. To say, if a business is a living system, which it is, how do we think so differently about the impact within that living system? It's because we are taught to think about things very silo, very mechanical. We have to change the way we think in order to have a different outcome, exactly what you are talking about. The joy of being part of this community is that we are all learning it together. It's too new for anyone to be an expert yet. That is so exciting to me to see a new way of thinking about companies and our culture.

Julie Ann: One thing I always tell companies that I work with, or if I am doing a presentation somewhere, silos are culture killers.

Sheryl: Oh my God, yes.

Julie Ann: I should just make a big road sign.

Sheryl: It's so hard to change because our models are so ingrained in us, especially if you have had a lot of experiences. It's like you've been bashed over the head that this is the way it works. Thank God for all of the new, younger people growing up, and hopefully we will start with a new approach to business as biology, instead of business as a machine.

Julie Ann: I like that as a living organism. Who comes up with all these great ideas that are connected? Do you have an open forum with your employees where they have the ability to say, hey let's try this? How does that work?

Sheryl: Yes. We always try to bubble it up from the company itself. Even from the days at Clif Bar®. I learned it means so much more. People are embracing it, they are coming up with the ideas, and they are seeing it live in the world. It allows them to tap into their passions. That's what makes businesses thrive, at the end of the day. I can talk about human trafficking all day long, but somehow that person has got to feel connected in a way that feels very personal to them. So let me give some concrete examples of things that we do. Our company is growing, and we can't always be in a room at the same time. But I didn't want to be like the culture edict. We have what we call a culture committee and each department is represented on the committee. We are just starting; we'll probably have someone stay on the culture committee for a year, then welcome new members, that way it is constantly refreshed. The whole idea is to get a pulse on the culture. What we need to do is make sure we are current and that we are always uplifting it. I love this guy David who is one of our sales managers who just joined the culture committee. Palo, our co-founder and I are always on the culture committee so we can help support the team. David comes into the group and he is just like this breath of fresh air. He asks about how do we inspire the passion of people, and offers ideas that he thought of, but without a place to put them. I'm getting to hear directly from David all these ideas and he is blowing my mind. I'm going to his sales leader and saying, "Chuck this guy is amazing." It turns out that Chuck had no idea this was going on in David. When you open up these avenues, it all comes out because people know their own essence. So much in business is about this person has these strengths and these weaknesses. Well, a lot of times we're the ones who have cultivated that. That limiting belief is not helping people to live to their full capacity of what's possible. To bring someone like that and put them in a completely different environment where they are free, gives you the opportunity to learn so much about the person, it also helps you be able to help them in their role. The culture committee is one example. I will tell you another beautiful example. Dani, who is our impact manager, and one of the people I was referencing earlier, she actually went to this conference called the Regenerative Business Conference. She came back and told me her mind was blown as to what is possible. This is Dani, she's a millennial, she's just in the beginning of her career, and she's telling me how we need to pay attention. She drove the whole thing. I'm like, right on, let's do it. I had no idea what this was going to be about. When the opportunity came about this community, I told Dani I'd love to introduce this to the company, but I can't do it until I really understand it myself. We met, this group of four of us, and we are called the Regenerative Explorers. We go into these community sessions so we can learn and bring it back to the company. It's another idea to think about. Sometimes in companies things get scary. It's something that is new to you as a leader, it's something new to people, but that shouldn't scare us. Let's have the boldness and humility at the same time that we go out and we learn, and we explore, and we test, and we try, and we have enough guts to say when something doesn't work. That's how we learn. We talk a lot in my company about bold humility as being a core of our value system.

Julie Ann: I think that's the only way it happens, right? I talk a lot about change, and people are always scared. They want to know, what's the change? What's going to happen? Well, you don't know everything in the beginning and, executing, I always say, is not the end of the line. That's the beginning of the next process. You execute, and then you see where to tweak, does it work or didn't work? A lot of pieces of business that change don't have to be in stone. They can be changed, or you can say we tried that and it didn't work like we thought it was going to.

Sheryl: It's an experiment.

Julie Ann: That's okay, that's the humility part, right? We screwed up, this isn't working, let's not put any more energy into it. But we learned X, Y, and Z, which will help us in some other endeavors. I think any time spent is not really lost, there is some value there, and it depends upon your mindset and your perspective.

Sheryl: I couldn't agree with you more. I have teenage boys, and it just makes me reflect every day on what you are saying because everything to them in this moment is the biggest deal, this is it.

Julie Ann: It's the end of life…

Sheryl: I just keep wanting to say to them, no, this is the next learning experience to the next stage, and life is going to go on for a very, very, very long time. It's not ending. It is hard in an environment where there is a lot of millennials. I'm sounding like such an old person, but I've been around for a while. The idea that it is just an experiment, it's all we are doing all the time. And if we are experimenting, we are learning, we are putting into place what works; we are taking away what doesn't or putting it in another place.

Julie Ann: And what's wrong with that?

Sheryl: Exactly. And that's what I love about the investors, for anyone who is working on companies with investors in it. Even they make the biggest difference in how much they support your approach. The investors that I have now, and I haven't always had investors like this that learn the hard way, but they also are willing to be vulnerable. They embrace humility; these ideas are talked about at every level of our company. Then, they turn around and support me as true partners in this way. For example, I just said to one of my investors right before this call, "I've been managing the month so closely, trying to make sure that everything comes exactly on the budget, but I'm making the sales team crazy. I need to stop doing that. I can't be on top of them every single month. I need you to support me. to not be looking at this in so much detail every single month." And he's like, "Right on, go for it." That opens us up to be able to focus on something else.

Julie Ann: That's a beautiful marriage you have there, and it's probably because everyone was up front and honest about what the goal is and everybody was on the same page. That's what makes a huge difference. Some companies use this podcast for recruiting knowing that the employee experience starts at the job board. They have people listen to it, and if they don't like the culture, they don't apply for the job. Wow, that's a lot cheaper for everybody.

Sheryl: It is so true. It's like a natural sifting system that is so incredibly true. I think you are right, it is a really good point for an investor to say, I'm willing to, at an early stage of the company, be okay with giving two-and-a-half percent of the net sales of every bottle to this non-profit. You've got to be a certain kind of investor to want to do that.

Julie Ann: Absolutely. And so that's why when you go to them and say I can't drive these people crazy anymore, they understand because they have the same mindset. We could talk for weeks, I'm pretty sure.

Sheryl: I think so.

Julie Ann: But, we are running out of time. So I want to ask you this before we leave. I am an entrepreneur, I am a business person, I'm a C-suite executive, I'm listening to this program and I'm saying well, I don't make drinks, I have a service, or I sell tires, or I'm in real estate. What is the one aspect of what you do that you believe any C-suite executive can utilize, regardless of what type of company they have?

Sheryl: I wrote a book about this called *Killing It: An Entrepreneur's Guide to Keeping Your Head Without Losing Your Heart*. In the book I'm just very transparent about the ups and downs that I've been through in my experiences as I felt like no one was talking about it. The big take away for me, after having some of the ups and downs I had, was I got lost between the difference in the net worth of my company and the self-worth I had. I equated these two equally. What I've learned and I think why my experience at Rebbl has been so deeply joyful is that they've learned how to separate those. It's not just important for family, or your friends, for yourself, or for the company. They all have to operate together. I realized too, that what I've learned from my family I bring into work and vice versa. I changed my title. My title is now the Chief Love Officer.

Julie Ann: I love it.

Sheryl: Everything needs to be grounded in love.

Julie Ann: I think that's a great way to end this for everyone who is listening, to remember that your net worth is not your self-worth. I love that. Thank you so much, Sheryl for your time today. I had a great time, and I'm sure we will be talking again.

Sheryl: Me, too. Thank you so much for inviting me.

Favorite Food: Big crunchy sweet green grapes

Hidden in this interview are ideas on how to handle too many priorities. Isn't this something we all deal with? The idea of identifying your essence is vital when choosing your priorities every day. Do you have a mission statement? Does it express your core essence, the reason you are in business in the first place? If all you are looking at is profit and not including people, then you might be in big trouble. I don't see that as sustainable in our current world. There is a lot of research to back that up. Watch out in the next 5 to 10 years as our employee pool shrinks.

At Rebbl, dedication to growth of the product, the people inside the company and the people who are an essential piece of their product, gives everyone an identifying lens to look through. If you spent five minutes with Sheryl, you would literally feel her passion. Passion throughout a company drives innovation and creativity. It creates a workplace, where not only do people want to show up, but they want to be there doing their best. They can see they make a difference. They are acknowledged that they make a difference and it feels good. Everyone wins!

People, Purpose, Profits & Play

with Chuck Runyon, CEO, Anytime Fitness

"When they're done with Anytime Fitness, I want them to say, "I worked at Anytime Fitness and I made the company better and Anytime Fitness made me better too."

Chuck Runyon

WHEN FISHMAN PR contacted me to have Chuck Runyon, the CEO of Anytime Fitness, on my podcast, I nonchalantly said, "Sure." I had no idea what a trend setting, award winning person my audience and I would get the opportunity to experience. In 2018 Entrepreneur Magazine ranked Anytime Fitness as the top-ranking global fitness franchise. Chuck Runyon was recognized by Chief Executive Magazine, with its Inaugural Leadership Award for his commitment to investing in people and relationships. If you know me at all, you are quite aware that I am all about ROR, return on relationships. It's what makes the difference between a flourishing, successful business and one that just exists. So, this award certainly got my attention. Specifically noted were Runyon's efforts to help his employees, not merely be more productive, but better people. I love that. Central to his leadership philosophy is the concept of R-O-E-I, the return on emotional investment.

CONVERSATION WITH JULIE ANN AND CHUCK:

Julie Ann: Wow you could be my next best friend Chuck.

Chuck's here to share with us the five people centric levels of his hierarchy to bring about corporate self-actualization. Did you read that book on self-actualization, "I'm Ok - You're Ok"?

Chuck: I did not read that specific book, but I've just been very familiar with the term.

Julie Ann I'm honored and it's a pleasure to be here. I think we have a shared mindset on employee engagement, so I look forward to our conversation.

Julie Ann: Well the first thing I want to know is, before you get into specifics, what was your aha moment or did you just instinctively know that if your employees were happy, your business was going to do a lot better?

Chuck: Over half our waking hours are spent at work. I think selfishly that I have always wanted to have a fun, enjoyable, productive and engaging environment. But I didn't really have to get as intentional about it until our business began to grow. Having that type of culture is really easy to do when you have got a really small team right? Five people, ten people...when you grow to twenty/thirty people, when your business is starting to scale past fifty and then you get past a hundred, then suddenly, you're in the hundreds of employees, you realize you have to be very strategic and intentional about engaging a much bigger workforce. You realize that you don't have the intimacy you used to have when you were a very, very small team. So, as our company was growing it really caused us to pause and say, look the small team organic stuff doesn't work anymore. We asked ourselves, how do we operationalize this philosophy? And, how do we broadcast this with the right cadence across all of our stakeholders? Not just to the hundreds of employees we have, we want to try and engage all of our franchise owners, four thousand strong across the globe. We want to give them that type of engagement and give them the tools, so they can do it in their businesses.

Julie Ann: Absolutely, and like you said, you have places, franchises all over the world so it's not like you can get everybody in the same room and get a message across.

Chuck: Yes, and today of course the irony is there are more ways to communicate, yet it's becoming more difficult because people are so crowded with information they receive every day. Part of my challenge every day is how do we communicate this? Whether it's verbally, with videos, with podcasts, with phones or you know with email, with live training events and so we are always trying to communicate the message of our core values to engage our stakeholders.

Julie Ann: Let's talk about your core values.

Chuck: Like many companies when we were starting to operationalize this, we got a big group together and pondered what our DNA words would be? We came up with twelve DNA words in our mission statement, vision statement. You know what though, I could never remember the twelve, no one could. I was like, there is a problem here, so we evolved and at the end of the day we settled with people, purpose, profits, and play, four words, everyone can remember. If you come to our corporate headquarters here in Minnesota, you will walk by two signs, one on the outside of the building, one on the inside of our building and they look like street signs. They just say people, purpose, profits, and play. We really try to work and live at the center of those four P's and for us it's about investing in people, being part of something that's bigger than ourselves and makes the world a better place. We know a business needs profits to thrive but let's have a good sense of fun at work too. So, we try to operationalize those four P's into our day-to-day business.

Julie Ann: And how do you invest in your workforce?

Chuck: We take half a percent of our annual revenue and we put it into an employee growth fund. Even when we were smaller we did this and now that we are larger we continue to do this. That growth fund can be used for personal growth or professional growth. I think that's what's different about our company. We have subsidized someone taking guitar lessons or running their first marathon. You know, doing something that has nothing to with their role in the business. What we value here is a culture of growth. The company's growing, we want you to grow, and we want you to stretch yourself. We always want everyone to have a growth mindset. How can we grow the business? How can we grow each other? Those funds can be allocated for both professional and personal growth. We put the money behind it and then we make the time for workshops during the workday for them to attend and learn new personal and professional development.

Julie Ann: That's a great idea, and I have talked to another business, a training company, and they sort of do the same thing. Everybody gets $2,000 to do whatever it is they want

Chuck: You know it's funny, that's kind of what we used to do. We used to take that half a percent and divide it up per employee. Then each employee could choose what to do and come back and share it. As we got bigger…

Julie Ann: You can't really do that.

Chuck: Well, it just became a little bit less efficient. We have what I call an employee council. These groups are the ones who are planning the parties and the workshops and the development classes. If someone wants to go off and do some professional accreditation, we still do the one offs. Our managers have the autonomy to do that, but really this employee group controls most of the spending.

They get to buy into it. They get to know what's part of the budget. They also get to report to the leadership team about how many people are attending and what the feedback and sentiment is. Half a percent of revenue, it's not much to invest into the training of your team and there's that wonderful adage out there that says, look the only thing worse than training your team and having them leave is to not train them and have them stay. Right? So, you have got to continue to invest in your people.

Julie Ann: Yeah, that is really true, and of course you're engaging them by allowing them to figure out what that means.

Chuck: Yes.

Julie Ann: Sometimes leaders get so caught up in giving orders all the time and not really allowing people to engage by engaging in their own company they are working at. When that happens, it makes a huge difference in how people work and how they feel about their work you know. People used to not want to talk about how people feel about their work, I started out talking about working happier and people would look at me like we don't want to do that [laughs] you know, they didn't like that word, happier.

Chuck: We have a lot of emotion in this workplace, we want our people to care, if they care, it means they're putting their heart into the business. It's okay if you laugh and it's okay if you cry here. It means you care about the business, it means you care about the impact you have on stakeholders, I think a great brand runs on EQ, high emotional intelligence and so we do not try to push that away, we try to endorse it and we want highly engaged, highly emotional people that are passionate in the business.

Julie Ann: Good for you, and I am sure you are richly rewarded with that. What is your turnover like in your business?

Chuck: It has been exceptionally low, even in the IT department, which, as you know, is very difficult these days to keep people. We have had a very low turnover over the last sixteen years since the inception of Anytime Fitness. If anything, we've probably had to let more people go than we've brought on because sometimes the business just outgrows certain roles or sometimes someone just doesn't have our values.

Julie Ann: It's not a good fit.

Chuck: Yeah, it's not a good fit. Otherwise our turnover has been pretty low. But more importantly, it's about high performance. You need a team to perform at a high level, especially in a competitive industry, to pull this company forward. To me, turnover is an area you really want to reduce the costs, but it's really about getting the maximum output, the maximum potential of the organization.

Julie Ann: Absolutely because it's not like you're the only exercise outfit around [laughs].

Chuck: Totally, yeah that's correct.

Julie Ann: So, you are always up against that and I think, in industries where there is competition and a lot of competition, the difference is how people are treated when they walk in the door. I mean everybody has treadmills, everybody has ellipticals, you know what I'm saying? And everybody has dumbbells, but what is the deciding factor? I stay in a lot of different hotels. They all have nice beds you know what I mean? They all have coffee machines in the room, they all have towels, but the difference is how am I treated?

Chuck: You are so right. One of the greatest strengths or benefits of our organization is when a local franchisee purchases an Anytime Fitness, their imbedded in the community. They care about their members. They care about their community and you really should feel that when you walk into an Anytime Fitness store. If they don't do that then you are right, we are just kind of an empty room full of equipment that has treadmills. Everyone can do that and therefore, I couldn't agree with you more.

Julie Ann: Well let's talk about your hierarchy of needs, explain first a little bit about what that is and what that means to you.

Chuck: When I try to categorize different types of businesses out there, I think about what most leaders fail to really give enough thought to. We worry all day long about our consumers, and how we differentiate ourselves. It's competitive out there and how do we win the wallet share of our consumers? I also put thought into our employees? How do we attract them? How do we retain them? How do we differentiate in a market that has got, right now, very low unemployment? Talented people can have their choice in where they want to work.

Julie Ann: And that's not going away anytime soon.

Chuck: No and so I'm looking at what's our competitive advantage to recruit people and retain people? We have a written employee value proposition, it is one sheet of paper that puts in writing how we differentiate, what you are going to experience here when you are an employee in our company, and we want to make sure that is a differentiating experience. We want to make sure we are better than the employer down the street. That is a mixture, of course, of compensation, you know things like benefits, but also our environment and everything we offer, including those reinvestments back into the employee. First and foremost, a leader has to think about how they compete for talent, and what their employee value proposition is, and they should write it down. It should be part of your strategic planning process. To help with that I wrote about the five types of companies. Level one is your standard pay and benefits. We've all had those jobs where we worked for an uncaring employer who really just bartered money for our butt in our seats right? They are renting your body, renting your mind, but you punch in, you punch out and they never think about you again. You really were a pawn. We have all worked for those companies. Then, we worked for the level two company, which is all that, but maybe better perks, you've got a nice workplace environment, they might have a gym on site, they've got a coffee shop and day-care…

Julie Ann: And a ping pong table.

Chuck: Yes, they've got some cool perks, but at the end of the day, you know, they are just a step above level one, but they're not truly getting you emotionally engaged in the work or in the business itself. So that's where level three comes in. This is a company with a purpose of, we do more here than just make money. We make the world or people into a better place. What do we do here? What is our product or service? How do we enrich others or enrich the planet? You want to get your employees to rally behind that, much like the famous Simon Sinek idea, then start with why? For us you've got to at least be a level three company to get the emotions going and then it's the reinvestment too. Take the money and reinvest it into your employees, and that's what we talked about before, we put our money where our mouth is and we want to invest in people. When they're done with Anytime Fitness, I want them to look back on their career and say two things. I want them to say, "I worked at Anytime Fitness and I made the company better and Anytime Fitness made me better too." Reciprocity. People are going to leave because there is another opportunity or they are relocating. I want them to feel like we made a difference in their life. If you do that, the fifth level is what I call the enlightened company, where a team is working so well together. It's about the work, not about egos. We collaborate at a very high level. We're all highly engaged. It's a very flat organization at the top. It's not about titles or hierarchy. Everyone is weighing in and there is a very healthy friction, but we trust each other. They can say, "Chuck I don't think your ideas very good." "Chuck, show me the data for that." Or, "I disagree with you." I mean, we tell people you should disagree with my partner and I. I don't care if you've been with us for three weeks, three months or three years, we want your perspective on this business and we want you to raise your hand and say, "Have you tried this?" "What about this idea?" "This isn't working." We really try to have healthy friction, healthy discussion in our company and if we can do that without ego, we don't care whose idea it is. You get to this certain enlightenment where the music becomes more important than the musician. We can make this beautiful music together, then we don't care who wrote the lyrics, we don't care who's got the guitar solo, and we don't care who came up with the idea, because all of us are making it better.

Julie Ann: It's the end goal.

Chuck: Yes.

Julie Ann: You are all in it for the same goal. Many leaders say they want that kind of healthy discussion, but people don't feel like they're in a safe environment to express themselves in that manner. That's where the problems come in. It sounds to me like you and your partner, and the rest of the leadership team, has built this kind of environment where people do feel safe to disagree. You have some humility is the word I am looking for. You're able to say, "You know what, I don't know everything. Just because I sit here doesn't mean I have all the answers." "I'm not in the gym everyday so I don't know all the good ideas that might come up from doing that." First of all, it's engaging, but it's also enriching. When you have your own humility, you can really be open to new perspectives, which can only make your company better and grow.

Chuck: I agree, and I would only add a bit of vulnerability as well. Because it's vulnerable for a leader to say, "I don't know this," or, "What do you think?" or, "That's a great idea." I think if you mix humility and vulnerability, it's a refreshing combination. I think your team enjoys the fact that we don't have all the answers and we're asking for their input. Really talented people want autonomy and they want to weigh in on something, even if they don't necessarily get their way. They just feel gratified because they're able to weigh in on it.

Julie Ann: Absolutely. It's that someone is truly listening to what they have to say. Their learning curve might be realizing that this great idea they had really wouldn't work for the company as a whole. If they are allowed to take that journey though, now they can understand that.

Chuck: That's correct.

Julie Ann: If they never get to do that, they feel like they just have to follow the status quo, even though they might have a good idea. So, that's a tremendous way to engage people in the overall goals of Anytime Fitness.

Chuck: I think in meetings you have to model this behavior, asking people what they think, asking them to weigh in and saying, "That's a great idea, have we considered this?" See who may agree or disagree. Ask, "What do you see from your angle of the business?" It's just having those open discussions. Look we don't need consensus, we don't need this to be unanimous, but we do want everyone's input to make the best idea possible.

Julie Ann: I like what you said too about leaving your ego at the door. I just love the people I am in a mastermind with right now because we care about each other enough to say, "That is not a good idea and this is why." We back it up and we don't feel threatened or hurt. We listen because we know it's coming from a place of caring for us and what we're doing in our business.

Chuck: So, Julie Ann it's funny because as we have gotten bigger, we have recruited talent from larger organizations that were very top down, that were very differential, so they have a tough time adjusting to the fact that in a meeting they can say, "I disagree with that idea, CEO," or, "I don't think that is the right thing we should do." Or, "Where's your proof on it?" "Where's your data?" It takes them like three, four, five months to really get comfortable and say, this is real, I can actually say this or question this. It's kind of funny.

Julie Ann: And, I would think you're not going to fire me or reprimand me or whatever.

Chuck: Exactly. They're not jockeying for politics or the bureaucracy. They really get in here and kind of don't let their guard down for a good 90 days.

Julie Ann: I'll bet because they are scared to death because of where they came from. As our employee base shrinks, which it is for many reasons and will continue to, people are going to take a job where they feel they really are a part of the whole. Not what you started this conversation talking about, you know, the level one. I just go to work I get my paycheck and I go home, nobody really cares what I think. People are not looking for that anymore. It's one of the things that the millennials did to business that I love them for.

Chuck: It's funny you mention that. I have often told people I am looking forward to the next era of leadership from millennials because I think they get this more holistic emotional purpose side of things. As they mature, I think it's going to be good for business. You're right, look if they are an "A" player they want to weigh in, they want their opinion to matter, and if they really do want just to barter for money, then you don't want them on your team. We don't want people here that are here just to punch a clock and do their work and get paid. We want your emotional investment. In meetings we don't only ask, "What do you think?" We also ask, "How do you feel?" "How are you feeling about the business? How do you feel about that decision? How do you think our stakeholder feels? I mean, weigh in on your feelings as well."

Julie Ann: And again, I think that goes back to vulnerability and that has become a bigger word in the C-Suite in the last year. Before then I never saw that word attached to C-Suite leaders. [Laughs] vulnerable, what? Be vulnerable? But now, more and more it is turning up in articles and Ted Talks and research, about how this is a vital aspect or characteristic in a good leader to be able to say, I do want to know how you feel, I do want to know when you disagree, so kudos to you for being able to do that.

Chuck: Thank you.

Julie Ann: Okay so, here are my listeners out there and they're saying, well I want a little bit of that. What would you say to someone who is building a company or even someone who has an established company? What would you suggest some of the first pieces of their business that they look at and first steps to take to turn around or go up to a different level?

Chuck: So, I've got two things that are absolutely immediate to me that really define top-notch leadership. That number one is if they have a level of self-awareness. This doesn't really start with the business it starts with you, right? How do others see you? How do you show up in the world with your nonverbal communication and your energy? What's the buzz about you? You have got to acquire some awareness. You can do this through some 360s. I just think you have got to be a bit introspective, how do you show up? What are your strengths and weaknesses? Now you can manage around that. That's number one, self-awareness. All of our great leaders have a level of self-awareness. Number two is your communication skills. And remember that starts with listening, right? So, think about listening first, especially as a leader. Think about being present with your non-verbal's, so they reflect what you're saying is so important to me, I'm not thinking about my cell phone, I'm not thinking about what I am having for dinner tonight, I am present in this meeting, I am present in this conversation. Then, your ability to communicate complexity, whether it's using PowerPoint Deck or using analogies, or just speaking clearly because everyone is feeling, you know, inundated with information. So, I'm telling you if you can be self-aware and have good communication skills, then you are going to find your way to success.

Julie Ann: It is so funny you say that because all my work in business culture and employee engagement starts with three Cs:

communication, collaboration and change management and communication is my key.

Chuck: Yes.

Julie Ann: It's not only a matter that I'm a big proponent of listening because you know, the word silent has the same letters as the word listen and I think there is a reason for that.

Chuck: I concur.

Julie Ann: It is important to have the mindset of truly being present like you said, to be in a conversation. Many times, I have coached people on how to set up those conversations. Awareness of where you are and what is going on around you is important. Maybe it's not the best time to have a conversation with somebody in a hallway. You might say, "I really want to be in this conversation, but I've got this project on my mind right now, so if it's not an emergency, could we possibly do it later?"

Chuck: That's correct.

Julie Ann: And it's interesting how many people...they just don't know the words to say. There are people that say, okay, we will have the conversation now, but it's really not a good conversation because they're not there.

Chuck: Yeah, so we've had some of those workshops I talked about, we have had a lot of classes around emotional intelligence, the ability to give and receive feedback. Some people, as you mentioned, are just unaware of how to do this. We do work a lot as a company on our emotional intelligence skills because it goes back to that collaboration piece. You've got to have high emotional intelligence to go along with your intellect.

Julie Ann: Absolutely. What you're doing and what I strive to do in my work is to make better people. That's what you were talking about.

Chuck: Yes.

Julie Ann: Better people have a better home life, whatever home life is, kids, no kids, spouse, no spouse, partner, no partner, it doesn't really matter, but everyone has a life away from work. If you can make that better, than you can make their work life better, because we now realize there is no separation from personal life and business life.

Chuck: Julie Ann, I want to reach across this podcast and hug you. We talk about that because we carry more phones and devices, so the lines between work and personal are blurry. We think if they are going to leave work happier and engaged, the rest of their life is happier and then they show up to work happier. That's why when we talk about personal growth we're like gosh if we can nudge them for personal growth outside of work and it makes their family life better or it makes their hobbies better, they are going to show up for work happier too. It's a full circle thing. Let's not just think about them in the context of work, let's look at them as a whole person to develop.

Julie Ann: Right, I heard somebody say, instead of work life, balance, which I think is an oxymoron, they said work life harmony.

Chuck: Oooh I like that better too.

Julie Ann: I think that's what it is all about, when I do my work in communication it's all about, how do you communicate here? How do you communicate at the grocery store? How do you communicate when you're on a volunteer committee? How do you communicate everywhere?

I do not let anyone say those are soft skills anymore, I always correct them and say really? I'm pretty sure they're essential skills because how do you get through the day without communicating?

Chuck: Could not agree more.

Julie Ann: What do I take as my first step if I'm looking to really make a change or I am just beginning? You said I should communicate better, be a little bit more vulnerable, and have humility. Anything else?

Chuck: Yes, you know I want to give the listeners a shift of mindset. This is critical because 99% of business leaders or owners would drive into work with the mentality of all these people work for me, and therefore it's like, what have you done for the business lately? I mean, you guys work for me and you have to report to me. I actually go in with a completely different mindset. I drive to work thinking I'm working for these people. It's my job to build them, help them and they will build the business. It doesn't matter if you have a business of three people, a business of three hundred people or a business of three thousand people, a leader should drive to work thinking, alright my first job is to these people at headquarters. How do I make them even better as humans or professionals at their job? If I build them, they will build the business. So, flip your mindset and drive to work every day saying, "I work for these people, they don't work for me."

Julie Ann: Wow, I want to come work for you.

Chuck: I promise you we will laugh, we will also work hard. By the way I want to make this perfectly clear, a great workplace environment isn't an easy workplace environment. I mean our people feel stressed, they feel deadlines, but "A" players and top performers want that. It's not easy here we tackle hard problems. But we still take the work seriously, without taking ourselves seriously. We still care so much it makes us cry sometimes. We can invest in each other and run a profitable business. So, you can achieve these four P's and love work.

Julie Ann: I like it and I think about how the world would be if everyone went to work and was excited about it.

Chuck: Oh, Julie Ann I don't know if you know this, the Gallop engagement study for the last ten years hasn't changed, seven out of ten people still drive to work not liking the experience.

Julie Ann: Right.

Chuck: That's miserable, we spend most of our time working and to think I would drive into work and not like it? So, selfishly I want to love my work, I want our people to love our work and as a cheap book plug people can order Love Work, which is our recent book we launched last year. It talks about the four P's. It is everything you and I just talked about today.

Julie Ann: Thank you so much Chuck, this has been very informative. I really like your take on employee engagement and business culture, and I really loved how you said it doesn't mean that you don't work hard. Some people out there still think if you're having fun then you're not working hard.

Chuck: No.

Julie Ann: In fact, I used to be an accountant in another life and I had a tax partner come to me once and tell me these words, "Well you are obviously not working hard enough because you have too good of an attitude."

Chuck: Oh, that is so sad. Look, there are days when I drive home and I want to pull my hair out, but I still love my people and what we stand for. It's not easy, but it can still be fun.

Julie Ann: Great, well thanks again for being with us and sharing your wisdom and expertise, I really appreciate it.

Chuck: Thank you Julie Ann.

Favorite Food: Sushi

Flip that organizational chart. Do you think people work for you or with you? That may be your first self-assessment. The difference in that mindset has much to do with how you treat those who support your company goals. This interview was all about the ripple effect of everything you do, and don't do, in building a company culture that breeds success. Chuck and his partner are masters at the realization that creating good humans, truly caring about the people *they* work for grows their business. And once again, how can you argue with success?

In conjunction with this self-assessment and opening up to your own self-awareness, is finding humility by recognizing your own areas that could use some reinforcing. Of course, you have to be vulnerable enough to be open to that. A part of emotional intelligence is understanding that the barriers to emotions, like humility and vulnerability, are mostly created inside you. You can choose to see those as positive qualities.

Follow the path of success with a foundation in communication. In all ways, to all stakeholders, and at all times. Be keenly aware of how you do this in every way you communicate, which includes, verbal, written and the non-verbal cues. Those are the ones that escape our own consciousness sometimes, but rarely those on the other side.

Chuck Runyon's Hierarchy of Needs to Survive and Thrive

Level 1: The Standard Pay and Benefits Company

Level 2: The Enhanced Benefits Company

Level 3: The Purpose-based Company

Level 4: The Reinvestment Company

Level 5: The Enlightened Company

Transparency, Reinforcement and Love = Success

with Catherine Monson, CEO, FASTSIGNS

"You always reprimand or coach in private and you praise in public."
Catherine Monson

Have you ever met someone whose presence captivates you in an instant? That is how I felt when I originally met Catherine Monson, CEO of FASTSIGNS® International. She is direct, has a powerful presence, and is wicked smart. I picked Catherine to include here because of her degree of transparency she has with her workforce. It's more than most companies I have worked with would be willing to disclose, but it is hard to argue with success.

Along with her hard driving attitude, she has a huge heart. She expects much and gives her team the tools they need to succeed. Too many times there are expectations in organizations with not enough support to really reach the goals. Not true at FASTSIGNS®.

Conversation with Julie Ann and Catherine:

Julie Ann: It has taken me almost a year, but that's because our guest is the amazing CEO of FASTSIGNS® International, Catherine Monson. She's been at the helm since 2009. Now, the International Franchise Association has awarded Catherine the Bonny Levine Award and the Fan of the

Year Award for her contribution to the growth of the business, her community, and promotion of professional advancement of women. Most recently, North Dallas Business Magazine named her top female executive. In her spare time, and I say that jokingly, she has appeared on the TV show "Undercover Boss," shared her expertise before the US House of Representatives, sits on several boards, writes for Franchising World Magazine, and is a keynote speaker. Today on Businesses That Care, we have the pleasure of her company, and I am so grateful you took the time for us, Catherine. Thank you so much.

Catherine: Julie Ann, it is my honor and privilege to be here with you.

Julie Ann: I want to start off by reading a quote from a blog that I found, and it was a quote from you that says, "Creating an engaging culture requires internal communication that is consistent and repetitive. Employee engagement reflects the commitment an employee has to his or her organization. The stronger the commitment, the more value can be derived through retention, public advocacy, and great performance." Wow, I couldn't agree more, and it's interesting, I do internal podcasts for companies, and one of the things I say is they create clear, consistent, concise communication, which is really, really important, as you pointed out in this. How do you do it?

Catherine: Well first, I happen to think that setting great culture is the single most important thing for any leader to do. Yes, there's strategy and that's important, but you could have great strategy and lousy culture, and you won't achieve anything.

Julie Ann: Right.

Catherine: In fact, I believe that culture eats strategy for lunch. I believe with great culture and mediocre strategy, you'll achieve a lot more than competitors or other companies that have great strategy and mediocre culture. So that whole thing about creating this workforce of team members who are empowered and involved and feel ownership in the business. I want everyone on my FASTSIGNS® International team to feel like they own this business. This is their business. It's not my business; it's not the private equity firm that owns us business. That culture creation, I happen to think it's 50% of my responsibility, right? I have to think it every day. I have to act on it every day. I have to reinforce it every day.

It started with defining it. I had to define what the attributes were that I wanted. Here are the attributes we're working on every day to enhance. We're open and positive, we act with passion, everybody on the team does the right thing, everybody on the team does what they say, and everybody on the team wants to execute with excellence and make it great. That's all encompassing. We have a value statement. We also have four key strategic objectives for the company, and they're simple, but every single one of my team members knows what they are. So I'll tell you what they are.

The first is to further improve franchisee profitability. We benchmark that every year. Next is to further grow average sales volume. For all of our locations, we're tracking what the average annual sales volume is and working to make it bigger. First, we're focused on profitability, then we think about increasing the value of the FASTSIGNS® brand and improving the already high franchisee satisfaction. As an example of that clear, concise communication, we have our core values and our strategic key objectives. They're simple, and they're straightforward. We have visual graphics around the office about it and everybody has a copy of it at their desk. Every single month, when we have our monthly company meetings we talk about both.

I ask for people to give me examples of how they've worked towards achieving one of those four key strategic objectives or how they have reflected our core values. And so I'm reinforcing it and I'm making people on the team say, "I helped a franchisee get this great customer." Or, "I helped a franchisee coach and counsel an employee for better performance." So they all understand how their particular job fits into achieving the four key objectives and how to wrap our values around their behavior. Not only do I do that every time I'm with my corporate staff, but any time I'm with my franchisees. Again, I don't have any meeting with more than a handful of us, without first reflecting on the four key strategic objectives and reflecting on the company values. So it's constant reinforcement.

Catherine: A big part of leadership is you have to lead by example. So what's so important about leading by example is to live it the same way. So if I'm asking my people to be open and positive and act with passion, and I act like a grumpy old hag, then there's no way we can say that I'm casting a good leadership shadow or-

Leading by example. I have to hold myself up to the highest standards, right? If I'm going to ask my people to do it, I better live it every single day. And everybody's human, and there may be some times where I drop the ball, in which case it's my job to own it. I need to say,

"Guys, I did not have a good day yesterday. I should not have said what I said. I take responsibility. I apologize." So this whole thing about leadership shadow or leading by example, I think is so critical because I set the tone. I may have things going on in my life that I'd rather have be different.

Julie Ann: As we all do.

Catherine: Right, but as I walk through the threshold of this business every day, I had better act with a positive mental attitude, right? We believe as a company that there are five common characteristics of all highly successful people. And the first and foremost of that is a positive attitude. We have a big long hall here and we call it the inspiration hall. And it has over 150 quotes about positive mental attitude, goal-directed behavior, self-motivation, a sense of urgency, and to never stop learning. We also share that list of 150 plus quotes on what it takes to be the best in all areas of your life with our franchisees. And now, as you enter FASTSIGNS® locations, and if you get back in the production area where the employees work, you're going to see these quotes on the walls of their production areas, because what are we trying to do? We're trying to feed the souls, the minds, and the spirits of all our employees. So, it's culture and it's helping everybody understand the simple strategic objectives of the company. It's helping everybody understand the core values, leading by example, and then it's involvement.

Every year we go through a business planning process, and we allow any employee that wants to be a part of it to be involved in that business plan, and once that business plan and that budget is put to bed, we share it with every single employee. At the beginning of every monthly company meeting, we're going through the eight objectives for the year and talking about our progress and where we are.

Another thing I'm a huge believer in is sharing the company's financial statements with employees. So every single month at our monthly company meeting, we share the prior month's results because we have to close the month. If you think about it, you normally don't get your financial statements done until about a tenth of the month, so our company meeting is soon thereafter. And we're talking about, here's what the revenues were. Here's what all the expenses are. Here are our earnings before interest taxes, depreciation, and amortization. Here's what our tax bill is. Here's the interest we're paying. Here's our earnings after taxes." So what I want my team to understand is, we're not making 99% profit. I want them to really understand. What happens when you educate them about the financial parts of the company? Things start happening like they turn lights off. They stop throwing away file folders that can be reused by putting a label on them. They stop throwing away paper clips because they understand how it all comes together.

Likewise, as we hit budget, each year we have incentives, like additional contributions to their 401k, right? So we're saying, "Help us hit the plan, help us be more successful, more profitable, and there's a reward for you." So all these things are aligned. We know, we get them involved, and then we empower them. We give them the tools and resources that they need to do their job. And if they feel they need a tool, a resource, they know to let us know because it's all about, "How do we empower you to achieve your specific objectives?" And then there's recognition that's thrown in there because we praise people. We work every day as a management team to catch people doing right, and then we praise them for it.

One of the things I do with every brand-new supervisor, is give them the book, the "One Minute Manager." I love the book, "One Minute Manager," by Ken Blanchard and Spencer Johnson. It's about catching people doing things right and praising them when you catch them doing things right. So, when they don't do something right, you can give them a one-minute reprimand without being harsh or negative., This gets them to tap into that desire to be the best. There's a bonus in then learning how to do one-minute goal setting. I think it all fits in together.

Then, I think there needs to be fun, right? We do fun things. We have fun events, we joke around in the company, we decorate people's offices, and we have crazy contests. For Easter we just had a bunch of jellybeans in a jar with a big prize for who could figure out the right number of jellybeans. We just try to do fun and interesting things. Every year we have, bring your family to work day, in the summer when the kids are off of school. We love having our employees bring their kids, their grandkids, their parents, and their grandparents into the building. We share with them what the company does and take them on tours. I teach the tour takers how to do it. How to walk them through the building, show them how we teach our franchisees to make money, explain what every department does and how important every department is. After that we have ice cream and cake, pop a shot and ping pong contests, face painting and a snow cone machine. We spend about three hours some July day, when everybody's out of school, just doing, bring your family to work day.

So we're trying to also have fun and help their family members understand how important their role is. Even our receptionist's family knows how important it is that she's here, that she's cheery, all the ways she helps us, how she interacts with customers. That just makes everybody feel appreciated and recognized.

There's another piece that I do, maybe it's because I'm a woman, maybe I'm able to do this better, and I'll try not to get choked up, but I will, and that's love. Everybody has hardships. I've got an employee right now whose wife was diagnosed with breast cancer. She had a lumpectomy a few days ago and had a bad reaction. He knows that he can come to me. I'm sending her cards and texts of encouragement and flowers. But it's more about checking in with him every day, "How is she doing today? Why are you here? Shouldn't you be home? I know you feel you ought to be here, but you only got one wife. Go home and be with her." So then there's this component that I just call love, and as you can probably hear in my voice, I get a little bit emotional about this.

Julie Ann: I'm emotional. It's connection, right? It's real honest connection.

Catherine: Yes, but I don't love them to get them to work harder. That's not the reason. I love them because they're people and I care about them and I want them to be the best and the happiest that they can be. I want to support them through those tough times, and I extend, if you will, that love to our franchisees. When I hear about a franchisee that's having a health issue or who just got married, or whose kid just got married or just had a baby, or just had a grandbaby. I want to share in that love and that recognition, so I spend a lot of time doing greeting cards and sending texts of encouragement and gifts. Because, I think all of that fits into creating a culture where we love our customers, we know the company's objectives, we know how to act and behave, we take accountability for our own personal results, we take accountability for the company's results, and we have fun while we're doing it.

Now, that's all easy to say, this rambling on I have just done for the last five or ten minutes, but it's the most important role. It's not easy to do; it's easy to say. It takes focus and commitment on the part of leadership. And then my direct reports know what our values are, and if I see one of my direct reports not living the value, I'm going to coach them about that. Never in front of somebody else because you always reprimand or coach in private and you praise in public.

Julie Ann: Right.

Catherine: But I'm going to hold myself accountable to our core values, I'm going to hold my direct reports to our core values. Then, they're going to hold their direct reports to our core values, and then we're going to celebrate folks that get good results and live our core values. It's that constant communication, and constant reinforcement, and connection that I think is the single most important thing that any CEO or leader can do. Create great culture and then you have to constantly reinforce it.

	In the absence of purposefully created culture and purposefully maintained culture, you're just going to get the culture of the lowest common denominator, right?
Julie Ann:	Absolutely.
Catherine:	Here's another thing we do, Julie Ann. If we have someone that no longer fits the culture, and sometimes that's because they can't recover from a life event, sometimes it's for some other reason, or maybe...
Julie Ann:	Just not a good fit.
Catherine:	Just not a good fit. We work to help them find a way to get employed someplace else.
Julie Ann:	But again, that's connection. That's a connection and understanding. That person then leaves still saying good things about who you are. I did an interview yesterday and that's how they felt. They want people who leave their company at some point in their life to say, "Wow, XYZ Company," or in this case, FASTSIGNS really made a difference in my life, even though I'm not working there anymore."
Catherine:	Another thing we work to do is training and develop our people. We might have a lunch and learn programs on how to read a financial statement or how to improve public speaking. Sometimes it's directly related to the jobs most of them do, and other times it's just for them. We've got one coming up on CPR and First Aid. Why? Because they may be in a situation where one of their family members needs CPR, and I want them to know how to do it.
Julie Ann:	Or one of their colleagues at work. You never know.
Catherine:	Yeah. I like to look at the whole person and I want to develop them. I've had many employees here that have

done great and then said, "I need more money for my family," or, "I'm ready for a promotion." We may not be ready as a company to give that to them, because we're not adding a thousand employees a day, right? We're managing our growth very, very well. I have many employees that have then found a position someplace else, and come back to me and say, "I learned more under your leadership at FASTSIGNS. I'm able to be a manager now with Samsung because of what you, Catherine, taught me."

Julie Ann: Right. That's exactly what I was saying.

Catherine: I heard this story one time about where somebody said, "If we train our employees, they may leave us." Then the flip side is, but if you don't train them, what's worse? What we also look at in one of our objectives when we talk about our annual business plan, is to train and develop our staff and expand them as individuals and give them tools and opportunities. If they outgrow the position we have for them today and we can't promote them in the time that's good for them, then let's let them go get a great job someplace else and still love us.

Another thing that's just a mindblower, Julie Ann, is I probably have nine people who have left the company and come back. And the story is, yeah the other company was going to pay me more money, but the culture sucked, and I hated it, and I wasn't happy. What that says is as long as we've got great culture, we hold people accountable for results, we give them the tools and resources to do it, we empower them, we recognize them, we have fun, and we love on them, if they leave us, they're going to always love us. They may very well come back because it was a great experience and that's all that's important to me as a leader.

Julie Ann: The research shows now, especially with the younger generations coming through, money is not the be-all and end-all to what they want. So, they are really looking for a culture they can feel a part of. I want to go back to a couple of areas, if you don't mind, that you talked about that I couldn't agree more with. One was accountability. When accountability is from the top down, that is so meaningful. You talked about coming back the next day and saying, "I'm sorry, I was in a bad mood. I shouldn't have reacted like that. In my consulting and coaching, I always tell people it is never, ever, ever too late to come back and say to somebody, 'Wow, I was in a nasty mood and that wasn't your fault, and I took it out on you.'"

Catherine: "That was my fault."

Julie Ann: Yeah. "'And I'm sorry.'" Because what you do to that relationship by saying, "I screwed up and I'm willing to tell you that and ask for forgiveness," is just amazing.

Another is your transparency It's a growing trend, but there's still a lot of resistance to do that. I just see the upside to financial transparency.

Catherine: So do I.

Julie Ann: You gave great examples. They use a file folder, they turn off the lights, they maybe even work a little harder and focus on one particular area because they want to see that number change on the financial statement. And because you give them such ownership with transparency, whether it's really all them or not, inside they're saying, "I had something to do with the sales going up."

Catherine: Exactly right. And then that makes them feel like winners.

Julie Ann: Absolutely.

Catherine: Which reinforces better work and better habits, which reinforces the culture, right? It all works together.

Julie Ann: Absolutely, and I love that you like to have fun. I love the idea of bringing the whole family to work. That's a new one. It's usually bring your kid to work or bring your dog to work, but I love the idea of bring your parents and bring your grandparents, I think that's tremendous.

Catherine: And you ought to see the pride on the employee's faces.

Particularly a young employee who gets to bring their mom and dad, and it could be an aunt or uncle, it could just be a next-door neighbor; we really don't care. It's whoever's important in your life. For them to understand the context in which this person works every single day is really, really fun.

Julie Ann: And you really know the importance of an aspect in life that I think of every day. We don't celebrate enough, and we need to do that, not only in companies, but also for ourselves. If you're going to make a checklist of things to do, then do your own little happy dance when you actually check them off. I actually do a happy dance sometimes, but even if you're just sitting at your desk and you say to yourself, "Yeah, I got that done."

Catherine: Well, I'll tell you what Julie Ann, as we're sitting here having this cup of coffee together, can you just show me that happy dance?

Julie Ann: Sure. No one else can see it, but, (Julie Ann dancing).

Catherine: Oh, I like it. Fantastic.

Julie Ann: You were speaking about your inspirational hall. I have an inspiration office and home. I probably have a hundred signs, mementos and keepsakes all over here reminding me of the person I want to be every single day. And to think that we don't need those kinds of reminders is just not true. Some people say, "If I need a reminder, then I'm not a good person, or I'm not really smart." No, it's just the opposite because I discovered a long time ago, it's the strong leader who can ask for help, not the other way around.

Catherine: Oh that's exactly right, exactly right. And I'm going to just add a cute story. It's a Zig Ziglar story.

Julie Ann: I love him.

Catherine: I love him too.

Julie Ann: I have his letter to me right back there.

Catherine: How special. So I'm going to have to tell you that I bought Zig Ziglar's house, so the house that Zig and Jean custom built 20+ years ago.

Julie Ann: I am coming to visit you.

Catherine: It has good juju.

Julie Ann: How could it not? And for the listeners who don't know who Zig Ziglar is-

Catherine and Julie Ann: (In unison) Google it.

Catherine: He was one of the world's best sales trainers and motivational speakers. Wonderful man. I had him over for dinner twice at my house and it was a sad day when he passed away, but I know he is in Heaven with angels. But Zig Ziglar was giving a big motivational speech one day, and at the end of a good speech you got a line of people that want to talk to you. And somebody walked up and said, "Well that's all well and good, but motivation doesn't

work." And Zig said, "Exactly right, and that's why we recommend it, just like bathing every single day."

And that's what inspiration hall is. Here's another thing I love to do with inspiration hall: when I come across a new quote, I just sent it to one of my guys on my tech team, he prints it on the adhesive-backed vinyl, he puts it in the hall, and we don't make any fanfare about it. Then, someone will come to me and say, "You added a new one." I said, "I don't know, prove it. What is it?" "Oh I saw, a diamond is a piece of coal that took stress really, really well." I said, "Exactly right. Good catch." It's fun when they notice something new in the hall.

Julie Ann: And that's what you want. That's better than you telling them. They found it and they come and tell you about it, all of these are ways to imprint that new saying to them.

Catherine: Exactly right.

Julie Ann: They read it and think, "Oh, no one told me about it." That's another imprint. Another accomplishment. Then, when they come and tell you about it it's another imprint. That's probably the sign they'll notice in the hall first for a while, because it's new. And then they'll tell somebody else about it.

Catherine: Yep, exactly right.

Julie Ann: Imprint, imprint. I love that. Okay, we're getting short on time, unfortunately. This has been wonderful and again, I so appreciate you taking the time to share what you know works. Let's think about my audience. I've got C Suite leaders out there that are a little slow to the train. They are coming around to, "You know what? I better get started on this business culture employee engagement idea." My advice is that as our employee base shrinks, which it is and will continue to do so, if you don't get on this train now, you're going to be late. My prediction, in the next five years is there's going to be many businesses shutting down because they can't get the employees they need to deliver their service or product. This dilemma is not like a small fire that you put out with a bucket of water; you can't do it in a minute. For those that want to get started, what would you suggest their first steps be? What do you think is most important? You've talked about so many great ideas; what do you feel is the foundation in these?

Catherine: I'd say the start is to sit down with your management team and decide on, in a couple sentences, 8 adjectives, what do you want your culture to be? I think first you have to define it in order to create it. It doesn't have to be polished, it doesn't have to be in complete sentences; ours is in phrases: Open and positive. Act with passion. Do the right thing. Do what you say. Make it great. And there's some bullet points under each of those like, be open and positive. Be fun. Be approachable. Be an active listener. There are some ideas underneath each one, which kind of describes what we're trying to create. Then, start sharing about it, and start celebrating your employees that live it. Then, have some succinct key objectives for the company, and then share them constantly. Then reward, recognize, and praise people who are doing things every day to achieve those key objectives and it all kind of starts to reinforce itself. That's where I would start.

Julie Ann: That sounds like a good beginning to me, and we are out of time. I have thoroughly enjoyed this. It was worth the wait.

Favorite Food: Sashimi

Does transparency work? I was working with a client who, like many, was reluctant to be financially transparent. I asked him to search for the answers to these questions: Figure out why you don't want to be? What is it you want to keep from your workforce? Imagine what it would be like if you shared it anyway? Catherine is willing to use her transparency and authenticity to create a workplace where people truly feel ownership. That makes people work with more care, creativity and commitment.

I loved hearing from Catherine about her understanding of repetition and reinforcement. When you have decided to create a flourishing culture, you first need to understand it is a continuous journey. There is no Thursday rally and we all work better together. Second, you must realize that reinforcement of those ideals comes from repetition. The more ingenious that repetition is, the more engaged your workforce is in it. Having the people most affected by these changes be a part of those engaging ideas, gets you way more engagement and follow through.

Last but not least, there is nothing wrong with loving your employees, truly caring for them and their well-being, shows up in leadership seeing the whole person. That's why Catherine knows what is going on in her employee's life, inside and outside of the office. That's why a part of their training is for them as human beings and not just how to do their job at FASTSIGNS® better.

Simple, but not easy. The need to make deliberate choices each moment is apparent.

FASTSIGNS.
More than fast. More than signs.

FASTSIGNS® CORE VALUES

BE OPEN AND POSITIVE	ACT WITH PASSION	DO THE RIGHT THING	DO WHAT YOU SAY	MAKE IT GREAT
Approachable	Be a Great Team Player	Honest	On Time	Execute with Excellence
Fun	Help First	Ethical	Finish What you Start	Play to Win
Level Headed	Confident yet Humble	Tell the Truth	Accountable	Continuous Improvement
Kind	For the Greater Good	Own It	Take Responsibility	Exceed Expectations
Empathetic	Make a Real Difference	Integrity	Punctual	Bring Out the Best in Others
Active Listening	Be Responsive	Compassionate	Communicate	Details Matter
			Follow Up	Innovate

The Magic of Maestro - What You Do Matters

with Sheryl Simmons, CHRO, Maestro Health

"We want to be your employer of choice not your employer of last resort."
Sheryl Simmons

AFTER I WAS ASKED TO JOIN the SHRM Blog Squad for their National Conference in 2018, I started going through the speakers to see who I might interview for Businesses that Care. I am always looking for women in leadership, since there are less of them, to keep my show balanced and my audience interested. Being a CHRO (Chief Human Resources Officer), I did a little research on Sheryl. I was not able to line her up for an interview before the conference, but did set up a time to meet with her at the conference. That meeting has turned into a friendship I cherish.

Sheryl is really smart and has a wicked good sense of humor. She is as authentic as they come. It is evident that she truly cares about every person in her workforce and every individual they serve. The old adage of walking your talk was made for Sheryl. Although, she is keenly aware of a National medical system that is broken, her goal is to make it work for their members. She utilizes Maestro's success stories to engage the workforce and make them profoundly aware of why they matter.

Sheryl focuses on the growth of each employee. She is protective while she nudges them to grow in new ways and is fierce about parameters, while being flexible to change. Wonderful combinations that make employees want to come to work and do their best.

CONVERSATION WITH JULIE ANN AND SHERYL:

Julie Ann: Today on Businesses That Care, we are interviewing Sheryl Simmons, the Chief Human Resources Officer at Maestro Health. When this airs, I will have already met Sheryl in person, at the SHRM National Conference in Chicago. Being a part of SHRM's Blog Squad, I went through the list of speakers and picked out only six people I wanted to interview, and you were one of them.

Sheryl: Wow. I'm impressed. Thank you.

Julie Ann: Thank you for being here.

Sheryl: Thank you Julie Ann, it's actually a privilege to be here, so thank you.

Julie Ann: It also says here that you're the Chief Compliance Officer, but we're not going to talk about that because, I don't like that name.

Sheryl: Yes, we need an exciting podcast, so let's stick with HR.

Julie Ann: The compliance, we know we have to do that, but let's stay with HR. There's a lot of HR departments out there that don't get to do the fun activities or instill the programs that you do into Maestro Health. It's so nice to know that Maestro Health thinks enough of their Human Resources Officer to say, "Build a culture, not just compliance."

Sheryl: Absolutely.

Julie Ann: To start out the show, I'd like you to give us a little bit of a background on how you got to be the Chief Human

Resources Officer at Maestro Health. Did you come in as the Chief Human Resources Officer? Or did you work somewhere else?

Sheryl: Tell you the story of Sheryl? Is that what you're after?

Julie Ann: Yes.

Sheryl: I've been in the HR industry for more years than I'm willing to give away, only my hairdresser truly knows how old I am. Back in 2013, even before that, the team here at Maestro knew what was coming on the horizon. US employers needed tech driven solutions. This convergence was coming of payers and partners and providers, and we said, "Let's get ahead of it."

Julie Ann: There's a concept.

Sheryl: Yes. Let's go to where the puck is going, versus them chasing it. And, that's why we created Maestro, back in 2013. We grew the company organically and then through acquisitions, I came on board as part of that acquisition. We purchased a TPA, (Third Party Administrator), we purchased a benefits administration, all of the components that you see we have built in our core products. We bought serious depth of talent and expertise to supplement the technology.

Julie Ann: Why recreate the wheel, right?

Sheryl: Exactly. So, I came on board as part of that. I was the Vice President of Human Resources at one of the companies that we purchased, Group Associates, and when my boss, the CEO, Rob Butler, approached the company, part of his requirement was that I be part of the deal. That's how much Maestro values what Human Resources bring to the table.

Julie Ann: Nice.

Sheryl: So, I had a conversation with him and we just clicked. We were and we still are absolutely on the same page about the importance of our employees and the culture and the value they bring. They are not Human Resources, they are the life and the breadth and the joy that we bring to the table for over 500 groups on our platform. Every day the people at Maestro get to participate in providing over a million people a day, tools and resources to live their best lives.

Julie Ann: What a great mindset.

Sheryl: We change lives every day across the United States, so what a great place to be a part of. That's how I came on to Maestro.

Julie Ann: Well, I love that. You know, I frequently talk about how important it is for people working in a company to know the greater purpose, their why. Why do they exist? What's the difference if they fill out this form or push this button or drive over here? It's a mindset that flows from the top down. It appears your mindset, which obviously moves into your entire workforce, is about having an opportunity to change lives.

Sheryl: And what a privilege that is to do every day and you talk about engagement when you know that what you are doing is changing and saving lives, it gives you a reason to wake up in the morning and go into the office or wherever you're working from that day.

Julie Ann: How do you allow everyone in the workforce to really know the difference they make? You can talk about a mindset and I'm sure there are different ideas that you have and actions you take within the company so people know they're changing lives. How do you really let them know? What is it that you do that's different so they can see directly how they affect other people?

Sheryl: One of the things is, Julie Ann, we share the stories. They're a part of our company. With client permissions and being careful to not share things outside of confidentiality and HIPAA, we share what we're doing. Four times a year, we do a town hall, our CEO, Rob, talks to the entire company and gives the State of the Union, here's what's going on. And we have the Rob and Sheryl Roadshow where we go out and we do fireside chats. There's just something magical that seems to happen when the CEO and the CHRO are sitting side by side and the employees have this thought that, "If Rob and Sheryl are both in the room, what they're saying is true, it's authentic, and we can believe in them." It just creates this sense of unity amongst the team.

I was just in Paris last week, talking about Maestro Health to a group over there. One of the stories I shared, was about one of our members, we don't like to call them clients or patients. These are people that we care about who needed to have a specialized injection for a very serious disease. And, specialized injections are astronomically expensive in the United States. Employers are being buried under the cost. A specialized injection for this member was just short of one million dollars which is mind-boggling. Through our platform and the algorithms that run behind the thousands upon thousands of claims that the system has its eyes on, it pops this out and says, "Hmm, a million dollars? Maybe we should talk about this?" It immediately alerts the Nurse Case Manager, who looks at it and looks to engage with the member and says, "The injection that you need, first of all that's what your doctor said, we honor that. They know what they're doing. But, if you have the same injection done at a very high-quality care facility just down the road..." look at the difference Julie Ann, one place it's a million dollars, this place is $600,000. We just saved $400,000 having both tech and customer care. So, then the next thing, the system triggers, is the Nurse Coach says, "Based on what we know about this person, I'd like to engage with them, because if we can coach them through a very manageable ten pound weight loss, their dosage drops."

Julie Ann: Oh wow.

Sheryl: We talk to the member and ask, "Are you interested?" "Yes, I'd really like to try that." So, we are positively coaching them through something that's very attainable, they drop the 10 pounds, the dosage drops, now we're down to $ 300,000. So, Julie Ann, just like that, we saved that employer $700,000 on one dosage in our very broken US healthcare system. When I can share that, when Rob can stand up and share that with our employees, they know what they do matters.

Julie Ann: Wow.

Sheryl: And we tell the stories behind it and we do those over and over again.

Julie Ann: That's great.

Sheryl: The magic of Maestro.

Julie Ann: I love the idea of having a town hall meeting. I love the idea of you and the CEO going out together as a unified front.

Sheryl: The dastardly duo.

Julie Ann: Do you guys ever come out in capes?

Sheryl: Oh, it's so funny that you mention that, because we're getting ready to move our Detroit office, and I had some things over there, and they found a big cape, a superhero cape that has HR on the back. On our communications channel, there was a message in all caps, "We have found Sheryl's secret identity."

Julie Ann: That is excellent. You have to work with people who have a sense of humor, right?

Sheryl: Life is too short not to.

Julie Ann: Yes. But that's an excellent story you told because, not only did you drop the price for the employer, but you have a patient who gets to lose 10 pounds that they wanted to lose anyway, with some encouragement, help, tools and skills.

Sheryl: And they get high quality of care. Win-win.

Julie Ann: I've never heard of any situation where somebody had the ability to have that information, that if they were 10 pounds lighter, they would get a smaller dosage. That's huge to have the ability to have that kind of information and the where with all to act upon it. To be able to work in an environment where you can come up and say, "You know what? I can help that person lose 10 pounds and they would have a smaller dosage and everybody wins."

Sheryl: In the platform itself, there's benefits administration that marries with population health management and benefit accounts. They all work together on the platform to give employees tools to lead their best lives. That's one of my favorite things about what we do. At the same time, to save significant funds of money for employers who value their employees, but have a P&L (profit & loss) to run, wondering how do I continue to pay for this cost? If I can walk in there and say, "I can give you both, are you interested?" And we're the only platform in the United States that has all of these products owned and operated by the same company.

Julie Ann: Under one roof.

Sheryl: Right.

Julie Ann: That's fantastic.

Julie Ann: Well, let's jump back to workplace culture. When you share these stories they certainly engage your workforce to continue to be a part of your team. There's no doubt about that. One of the things that I was looking at when I was doing research on you, was the fact that you not only encourage people to grow personally and professionally, but you have your eye out for someone who may be a great employee, not just a good fit in what they're doing. And so, instead of tossing them to the wind, you work with them and find out maybe if there's someplace else they would be good at. So, talk to us a little bit about that.

Sheryl: Absolutely. Let's look at it from business strategy. We invest a lot in time and money to bring talent into the Maestro family. So, as HR and executive sponsorship, lots of money is being spent. So, I've already vetted them. Of the top three things we're looking for in candidates for Maestro Health, the absolute number one is are they a good cultural fit? That is a knockout question for us. Then, it's talent, which is the ability to learn more and then your skill. What do you know, what do you bring to the table? That's the trifecta, but Julie Ann, it's in that order. You have to be a good culture fit to be successful with Maestro. In the market where we're at right now, in many sectors there's under employment. People are fighting for talent. So, you get folks in the door, and you realize their skillset may be different than what they thought it was. Or what they thought they were coming to do is a little bit different than what they heard.

Julie Ann: Or they may think they want to do something, but never really worked at that, and once they get there, you know, it's really difficult. Where my son went to school, the kids who wanted to go into pre-med, went into the operating room in their senior year at a local hospital. Well, they may think they want to be pre-med and they may get in there and go, "Blood?"

Sheryl: And pass out, right?

Julie Ann: So, maybe that's not a good fit. Right? I'm using that as an extreme, but it's the same thing. I love marketing, I love sales, I love taking care of the elderly, whatever it is you think you like to do, until you do it, you don't know.

Sheryl: You don't know what you don't know.

Sheryl: So, these terrific people come into the Maestro Health ecosystem, and they're terrific cultural fits, they have the talent to learn more, they have the base skillset that they came in with, why would you not help them curate their best career?

Julie Ann: Love that word, curate.

Sheryl: Why would you not encourage them to do what they love and continue to up skill them? Because everything they're learning and doing brings strength and diversity and engagement to the company. So, besides the brick and mortars, we have employees all over the country, I am all about wanting Maestro Health to be the best gig you ever had in your career. We say, "We want to be your employer of choice, not your employer of last resort."

Julie Ann: That's good.

Sheryl: And you know what? Sometimes people don't work out, for a myriad of reasons. You know, they'll go find their passion somewhere else. Sometimes after we've curated and grown them and they've reached as far as their potential is going to take them here, they go on to their next career adventure People are often shocked at Maestro when we celebrate that with them. And they're like, "You're not upset that I resigned?" Well, of course, I hate losing fantastic employees, but who in the room has never quit a job to move on to their next thing? It is such an honor to grow them and be part of their journey, and they move on and who knows, down the road, I may have something open up that they're a perfect fit for. They're going to come right back, because this is their best gig, or they're going to send me somebody they trust, that they know. I believe in them, and we're passionate about helping our staff to be their very best selves.

Julie Ann: See, I knew you'd be perfect for this show, because that's exactly the kind of people I talk to on this podcast, people who understand that this is a whole journey. The words employee engagement, as you probably know are changing now into the employee experience. Employee engagements are old school now.

Sheryl: It's going to be the old word.

Julie Ann: It was kind of like wellness and then we had well-being. Now we have employee experience, which is what do I experience when I see that job for the first time on the website, to what happens to me when I leave? And, you're the epitome of that. We celebrate that you're going to find something else and maybe it'll work for you and maybe not, but we want you to leave here with a good memory, not a bad memory. We don't want you to leave and say, "Oh Maestro was the worst place I've ever worked." We want you to say, "You know, it didn't work out, but gosh that was a great place to be. I hope something shows up later so I can go back there."

Sheryl: I want them to have reached their absolute full potential, for every position that I have open that they have a passion for. And, when they have fulfilled all of that, if there's nothing left for Maestro to offer them, to launch them to their next adventure.

Julie Ann: I think that's a great idea!

Sheryl: When they come in, we also tell our new hires, "Listen, for the first 90 days, you are going to bring a gift to us, and that is the gift of a brand new perspective on what we're doing. So, you can see with a fresh set of eyes, does this make sense? Do you have questions? Have what we told you you're going to be doing translated into what you're actually doing? When you're looking at our delivery and our products and our services, what do you have to share with us, because you haven't been in the trenches with us for however many years? Share with us your perspective and your feedback."

Julie Ann: Oh, you'd hate me as a new hire. I'd have like 900 ideas.

Sheryl: No, actually you would be of great value, because it would be, "You know what? We didn't think of that." Or, if you presented it, and I said, "Well, Julie Ann, thanks for sharing." Then I would be able to help you understand more of what the Maestro journey looks like, right?

Julie Ann: Here's why it wouldn't work right now.

Julie Ann: What a wonderful entrance into a company. I was just talking to somebody earlier today about how many times people don't feel safe at any point in their career in a company, to speak up and of course that's why we have these big recalls because people aren't willing to speak up.

Sheryl: Absolutely.

Julie Ann: Or they don't feel they can, or they're worried they're going to lose their job. So, you're doing just the opposite, you're taking them when they come in and saying, "Oh, we want to know what you have to say."

Sheryl: Raise your hand.

Julie Ann: Yes, raise your hand. This was a great way of onboarding. If you're missing something and we're expecting you to know it, if you don't tell us, we don't know.

Sheryl: We don't know what we don't know.

Julie Ann: Yes. And we can't fix it because we don't know it's broken.

Sheryl: Therefore, share your experiences with us. I say there's a shared pool of knowledge, and we all get better by everybody contributing. However, when people don't contribute to that shared pool, that is how a large group of smart people make stupid decisions. And, that's what raising your hand is about. Everybody from the CEO, to the person who cleans up the office in the evening, and everybody in between, is charged with raise your hand. It's a job requirement, raise your hand, and we want to hear what you have to say.

Julie Ann: I like that. And, you know, much of the time, if people feel like they can say something, it doesn't even matter if you agree, it doesn't even matter if the idea will work, it's the fact, wow, someone is willing to listen to what I have to say. Now I'm valued.

Sheryl: You create that safe space so they can. For them, it might be a great act of courage, especially if they have come from an environment that is not like Maestro.

Julie Ann: Or a life like that.

Sheryl: Right. What you're saying is, you care what I have to say, and everybody in the room is nodding and saying, "Yes. Yes we do. What you have to say brings value to the organization."

Julie Ann: And I'm sure you have people coming in who haven't seen that in their life, haven't experienced it, whether it be in their personal or professional life or both, and it probably takes them a little while to feel like you're serious.

Sheryl: This is real. We've had new hires, you know, into the journey, and they'll come back and say, "I didn't think it was going to be what you said, or at least not as good as you said. Not only is it everything you said, but also you've delivered everything you promised. The culture that you've described is exactly what it is at Maestro." And again, huge compliment for us, because we know we've delivered a communication that they have heard what we have said. So, the understanding is going both ways, and for us, that means we've just hit it out of the park.

Julie Ann: And not only that, but I am sure that that shows up in your low turnover rate as well.

Sheryl: Yes. One of the things we measure is, regrettable attrition, which is, they have left and it's breaking my heart because they're leaving, our regrettable attrition is under one half of one percent.

Julie Ann: Wow.

Sheryl: That's big.

Julie Ann: That's fantastic.

Sheryl: It's important for companies to have turnover so they don't stagnate.

Julie Ann: Right.

Sheryl: But, it's a combination of not stagnating and making sure you have the right talent at the time.

Julie Ann: Well, like you were talking about before, some people have to leave because you don't have a spot for them, doesn't mean they left because it was a bad experience.

Sheryl: One half of one percent of regrettable attrition is an amazing thing.

Julie Ann: All right. I want to spend a couple more minutes on how you encourage people to grow personally and professionally, because I know you have some unique ideas in that area.

Sheryl: Well, you start by creating that space, so that they realize you're serious and that you have their best interests at heart. Any opening that we have at Maestro is posted on our website, full transparency. If they're interested in another position or location, we encourage them to talk to someone about it. Maybe they are sitting in HR, looking at sales and realizing their favorite thing to do is promote this company. They are encouraged to go have a talk with marketing. Figure out what your passion is, and if you need help with that, let me know. I coach and mentor people all over the company, they call it Sheryl Time, where you get 25 undivided minutes of my time. You do homework the night before, and we have conversations about your career and what you can do to grow yourself at Maestro. And I'm not the only one. That is pervasive in the Maestro culture.

Julie Ann: Excellent. Before we leave, because this is such an important topic, I know Maestro has a great focus on gender, race, religion, and sexual orientation, all of these areas in which there seems to be great gaps in many companies, and you do a lot of work to not have those gaps.

Sheryl: Absolutely. And, the funny thing is Julie Ann; I had the CEO of a huge recruiting firm come visit me here at Maestro. She walked around and said, "Sheryl, I'm blown away by the number of women you have in tech, and that you create this diversity initiative and policy to do that." And I said, "Megan, I have to fess up, in the spirit of truth, we don't have one." She's like, "What do you mean?"

Sheryl: I said, "Here's the thing. When you focus on the talent, and your only objective is to find the exact right person for that job, you don't care what the package looks like, you don't care about race or gender or identification. It's not of an importance to us, instead we celebrate it. We joke and say I don't care which your feet face in the bathroom stall, I really care about what you do here at the office." I am a coffee junkie, it's a given, they tease me about it. And I tell people, "Picking your talent by the package is like picking your coffee based on the coffee mug. It makes no sense whatsoever."

Julie Ann: I like that.

Sheryl: We have just an incredibly diverse population of employees here. Because of that and their backgrounds, they make the magic of Maestro.

Julie Ann: The extra benefits to having that diversity in a company is for everyone because there's probably people in your company who haven't been used to being around a diverse population. So, you're really giving those people an opportunity to experience people who are different. We all know that problems arise mostly because people aren't educated about these differences. Perhaps they've never been around somebody who's a different race. They've never been around somebody who's a different religion. They've never been around somebody who's of a different sexual orientation. You are providing an environment where people can experience people that are different from themselves.

Sheryl: And celebrate it.

Julie Ann: Absolutely. I love that picture of what you said to me before, "We don't care which way your feet face in the stall."

Sheryl: That gives you a little insight to Maestro humor. We are a tad bit irreverent, and we have a lot of fun. We are so inclusive, but the one area we are exclusive is if you don't live and breathe our values. If you don't live and breathe our vision and our mission, I don't care if you are a superstar, I will invite you to showcase your talents elsewhere. Because the team we have curated here, what they do every single day, I am not going to do anything that puts that in jeopardy. That's why you make sure you bring the right people to the table, who are passionate about what we're doing, that care deeply for each other and know that we are their second family, because your first family always comes first at Maestro.

Julie Ann: Well, that's a good way for us to end. Thank you so much for sharing your great ideas. We have a saying here, simple solutions give you big results. And you have certainly shared several solutions that don't cost money to implement, but they make huge differences in the workforce, your culture and the way people go home every day just a little happier.

Sheryl: Absolutely.

Julie Ann: Thanks so much Sheryl.

Sheryl: Thank you. It was a joy to talk to you.

Favorite Food: A bone-in ribeye, medium rare

Wanting to be the employer of choice, instead of the employer of last resort, takes a lot of forethought, continuous improvement and resolve. It is more than what you do it involves how you think. This process starts at the top. Sheryl is blessed to be able to work with a CEO who is aware of the same keys to success as she is. There is an intrinsic understanding that by creating a culture where people are welcome, given plenty of opportunities for growth and even celebrated on their way out, the entire cycle will benefit. Greater talent comes in, higher quality work is achieved, your client is better serviced, and your bottom line grows. It's not rocket science, but it does take deliberate choices...every day.

Sherly starts with making the number one priority in hiring, a good cultural fit. That means you have to be transparent about what your culture really is. Then, you have to be vulnerable enough to ask and find out if what you had intended is what your new employees experience really is. Can you do that? No one said it was going to be easy, but like any habit, the more you practice, the more you look at your organization with a different lens, the easier it all becomes. Everyone benefits.

How to Create A Purposeful, Passionate Tribe

with Garry Ridge, CEO, WD-40

"Purpose-driven passionate people guided by their values create amazing outcomes"

Garry Ridge

THE TITLE OF THE ARTICLE in Inc. Magazine was, *"WD-40 Does $380 Million in Sales a Year. Its Secret Sauce Is Surprisingly Simple."* After reading through it, I went on LinkedIn, reached out and asked Garry Ridge if he would consider my podcast. His answer was, "G'day. Let's chat." From that moment forward and throughout our conversation, he was so easy to talk with, very matter of fact and authentic. I seriously wanted to work for him after our interview.

The philosophies of how they create their company culture reminded me of my friend, Steve Wilson. He taught me that change can be simple, but not easy. At WD-40, their values and ideas are simple, most don't cost dollars, but they do take determination and making conscious decisions every day. For quite a while now, I have realized that to build a thriving business culture, you must build processes into the fabric of organization. Garry Ridge and his team have done this so well.

Just read their Maniac Pledge. It says, "I am responsible for taking action, asking questions, getting answers, and making decisions. I won't wait for someone to tell me. If I need to know, I am responsible for asking. I have no right to be offended if I didn't get this sooner. And if I'm doing something others should know about, I'm responsible for telling them." That's why we say, at the company we don't make mistakes, we have learning moments.

Read this, take notes, and implement their ideas…if you want to be successful.

CONVERSATION WITH JULIE ANN AND GARRY:

Julie Ann: I am honored and pleased to have with me Garry Ridge, who is the CEO of the WD-40 Company. Now, I don't know about the rest of my listeners, but I never have a home without WD-40 in it. WD-40 and duct tape. You can do anything almost. That and a screwdriver, right Garry?

Garry: Absolutely. Good day, Julie Ann. How are you?

Julie Ann: I'm good. Thanks so much for joining us today. I was reading about you and saw you have been the CEO since 1997. I see you're also an adjunct professor at University of San Diego. I lived in San Diego for a while. It's a beautiful place out there. Your business has really grown since you came on board. Why don't you tell us a little bit about that?

Garry: We're very lucky that there are lots of squeaks in China and lots of rust in Russia, and we're just the boys and girls to take care of that. Certainly our goal 20 years ago was to take the blue and yellow can with a little red top to the world, and we've been busy doing that for the last 20 years. Now, we have our product in about 175 countries. We make it in 20 countries around the world. And we continue to solve problems every day by creating positive lasting memories in workshops, factories, and homes around the world.

Julie Ann: When you said, "Creating positive lasting memories by developing and selling products that solve problems.," I thought what a great way to have everyone in your company understand its greater purpose. When I speak and consult on culture, I emphasize how important it is that everybody knows what the purpose is. Not the purpose of what their job is on a daily basis, filling out forms, making sales, etc., not that, but the greater purpose. It sounds to me like that's something that definitely flows through your entire workforce.

Garry: I truly believe that. I am convinced that purpose-driven passionate people, guided by their values, create amazing outcomes. I love some of the work that Simon Sinek has done. Simon is a dear friend of mine and I love it when we can say, "Think about a place where you go to work every day. You contribute to something bigger than yourself. You learn. You have fun. And you go home happy." Really, that's what we deserve to deliver to the people in our organizations. So many people today, in fact about 66% of people, go to work every day and are either disengaged or actively disengaged.

Julie Ann: Those numbers haven't changed very much in the last 10 years.

Garry: Well, they haven't changed much since 384 BC. In fact, Aristotle said in 384 BC, "Pleasure in the job puts perfection in the work." And I guess we're just very slow learners.

Julie Ann: Sometimes in my research, finding things on the Internet, and reading different articles, somebody will use a quote by Plato or Aristotle, and it's completely relatable today. These aren't new ideas or new issues that we've had in life. We're just finally getting around to thinking, you know, that's probably a really good idea. We should work on that. I love that idea of greater purpose. Are there things you do within your company so that people constantly know about that purpose?

Garry: There are a couple of things. Firstly, it's something we talk about all the time so people understand. If you asked anybody in our company, "What is our why?" Why do we get up every day?" They'll share that purpose with you. It's the cornerstone of building our culture, which is a culture where people are treated with respect and dignity. They understand and value the power of belonging. One of the biggest desires we have as human beings is to belong. And a lot of organizations probably go out of their way, possibly unintentionally, to not create that feeling of belonging. In fact, my friend Ken Blanchard says, "It's a shame that the only way that most people know they're doing a good job is no one yelled at them today." There are so many things that we do as leaders that suck the soul out of people and that's not fair. So yeah, we live our purpose every day. We're set free by our values. We have a tribal culture, which is about learning, and teaching, and values, and belonging, and celebrating, and being warriors. All of that together does build a positive culture where people actually want to go to work. In fact, in our latest employee opinion survey, we've been doing these for 20 years by the way, the highest ranked answer, at 99% from our global tribe, said they love telling people they work at our company. That's something that gives me peace because if they love telling people they work at the company, they're going to take care of our customers. If they take care of our customers, our customers will take care of our stakeholders.

Julie Ann: That's the way it works. It's unfortunate how many companies out there still don't get that.

Garry: Many don't get it.

Julie Ann: Because your best customer is your workforce.

Garry: Absolutely.

Julie Ann: If workforce isn't happy, how are your customers going to be happy?

Garry: They're not going to be happy. And we've all experienced that many times. We go out, and interact with organizations that use the, "It's not done that way," or "It's not our policy." duck. You go in and you ask, "Can I do this?" "It's not our policy." And, "We don't do that." And if you complain enough, you then go up to the head mallard, which is the senior leader, and he just has a louder quack, and it's because we're not giving people freedom.

Julie Ann: One of the important things I heard you say was how you give the people in your workforce respect. And I know from experience that when people are treated with respect, they're more apt to give respect. Not the other way around.

Garry: Totally true. I mean our foundation is based on care, candor, accountability, and responsibility. And in an organization where we say, "We care about you." It's not just the tenderhearted. It's sometimes like a parent. Caring is being both tough-minded and tenderhearted. We've got to, as a caring organization, make sure we have a great plan, and that we have the resources. We only have time, talent, treasure, and technology and none of them are abundant. It's our responsibility as leaders to ensure we're using those assets in the best way we can. Candor in our organization is pretty simple. It means no lying, no faking, and no hiding. We have a pledge in the company that we call The Maniac Pledge. And it says, "I am responsible for taking action, asking questions, getting answers, and making decisions. I won't wait for someone to tell me. If I need to know, I am responsible for asking. I have no right to be offended if I didn't get this sooner. And if I'm doing something others should know about, I'm responsible for telling them." And that is really a pledge of responsibility and accountability to each other.

Julie Ann: I'm all about accountability. Many times my audiences are a part of the workforce. They're not management. They're not in the C suite. And I say, "Hey, it'd be nice if management did X, Y, and Z for you, but you have to do it for yourself. You can't always wait for someone else to do it for you." That's a bonus if that happens, but you have to learn how to celebrate your own successes in life. You can't always wait for somebody else to pat you on the back.

Garry: No, life is a gift. Don't send it back unwrapped.

Julie Ann: Yeah, I know, absolutely. That's funny. I used to have a holiday card that went out years ago. And it said, "Life is a gift. Rejoice in it."

Garry: There you go.

Julie Ann: I get up every morning happy for another day. So, I totally understand how that works. I like that Maniac Pledge a

lot. And I love the other idea of care, candor, and what was the last one? Accountability.

Garry: Care, candor, accountability, and responsibility. The Four Pillars of the Fearless Tribe.

Julie Ann: And responsibility. Yes. It's interesting you were talking about having a tribal culture. And I wonder if that comes from your Australian background?

Garry: Well, the attributes of the tribe were from some study that we did after we were talking about teams and tribes many, many, many, many years ago. If you accept the fact, as Maslow talks about it in his Hierarchy to Self-Actualization, the first two runs of that journey are sort of survival and security, and most organizations give you survival and security. The next one is belonging. A lot of people in organizations talk about belonging to a team. And when I thought about belonging to a team, I thought about when I was in high school in Australia. I played rugby on a team. Was that fun? Yes. What was the team's objective? The team's objective was to win an identified game in a specified period of time. In the game of business, our job is really to build an enduring company over time. Although, you had teams, what we really wanted to do was have a tribe because if you think back over thousands of years, we're very tribal as individuals.

Garry: I wondered, what made these tribes succeed back thousands of years ago in harsh conditions? So I went back and I looked at what the tribal attributes of the Australian aborigines and the Fijian Islanders were. I came out with that in both circumstances, there were attributes that were very similar. The first attribute of a strong tribe is the leader being a learner and a teacher. If you think about going back thousands of years ago and you're at a meeting of the Australian Aborigines, in the middle of the Australian desert, the tribal leader would be teaching the young tribe members to throw a boomerang. If any of your listeners have ever tried to throw a boomerang, they know it's not easy. Back then if you couldn't do it, there's a chance you wouldn't survive because it was the hunting tool of the time. So it became obvious to us that to be a tribe, which is something that builds an enduring culture over time, the biggest, important thing was for the tribal leader to be a learner and a teacher. And so, yes, back to your original question, there is some connection to my homeland.

Julie Ann: I like that aspect of learning and teaching because there is a piece of humility in there and a piece of caring. When you're teaching, you're caring. You're sharing your knowledge with others. My company's name is Learning Never Ends. I'm all about continuous learning. When you're learning, there's a bit of humility in you that says, "I always have something more to learn."

Garry: Oh, I'm consciously incompetent and I learned three very important words many years ago.

Julie Ann: I don't know?

Garry: I don't know. They're my three most powerful words. And getting comfortable with them is very, very important.

Julie Ann: I have a friend, Jeffrey Hayzlett, and in my book on employee engagement, I use his famous quote, "I don't know what I don't know." He was sitting in a big meeting and people said, "You can't ask that question." He was a

CMO at the time. And he said, "Why? I don't know what I don't know."

Garry: Exactly.

Julie Ann: "I don't understand what they're saying. How can we negotiate this deal?"

Garry: It became very clear to me, maybe 20 or more years ago when I first moved to San Diego from Australia. I hadn't been in this country long and was a director of some of the company's international business. I was sitting in a meeting with some other colleagues there was someone giving a presentation on a subject. About 15 minutes into this presentation, and what was going through my head was, I have no clue what this person is talking about. So, I said to myself, okay, well, I'll go out on a limb here. I put my hand up and I said, "I'm sorry, but I don't have any idea what you're talking about." And everybody in the room went, "Ah."

Julie Ann: Because they didn't know either.

Garry: Because they didn't know either. It was just that I was the dumb Aussie who was brave enough to ask.

Julie Ann: Oh, I've been a question box my whole life. All through school, after class, my teachers would say, "Thanks so much for asking all those questions because every time you did, four other people were nodding their heads, going, yeah I want to know that too."

Garry: Exactly. I learned a long time ago that it's really the power of the people that you surround yourself with and giving them the opportunity to step into the best version of their personal self every day and letting them experiment. That's why we say at the company we don't make mistakes. We have learning moments. And we say that because early on it was very clear that people were very, very shy about talking about what you would call failure. So we said, "Let's take the word failure out of our vocab. Let's replace it with the learning moment." And now we celebrate positive and negative learning moments. Our definition of a learning moment is a positive or negative outcome of any situation that has to be openly and freely shared to benefit all.

Julie Ann: And that's exactly what I was thinking as you were talking about that. When I have a learning moment, instead of calling it a failure, I realize I am actually learning something new about myself, the project I am on or a new way to deal with a client or customer. My experience helps everybody else so they don't step in that same hole.

Garry: As long as you're brave enough and the company has put in a culture where it's safe enough to speak up. Safety is so important.

Julie Ann: There are too many companies, unfortunately, where people don't speak up because they don't feel they're in a safe place. I discover that a lot when I talk with leadership and they say, "We have this particular issue." Then, I'll take an anonymous survey of the workforce and discover they have an entirely different issue, or the issue is much bigger than they thought.

I'm willing to bet, Garry, that you're one of those people who is a leader by example. I would put money on it that there has been times when you have shared a learning moment with your workforce as well.

Garry: I have an abundance of learning moments. I'm not at all embarrassed or shy about showing my vulnerability. I'm just a simple, basic guy bumbling down my road of life, bumping into stuff. I'm very comfortable with admitting when I screw up. One thing that's important to our organization, that gives people this trust is our values. Each of our values has a definition written so people understand what they mean. One of them is doing the right thing. We say that if people make decisions in our company and they do it by respecting and living by our values, nothing bad can happen. The decision may not be optimal, but I'll tell you, as long as they say, "We looked at our values. We said we're doing the right thing. We created a positive lasting memory. Our action was really there to make it better than it was today. We really did it so we would succeed as a tribe and we would excel as an individual. We're going to own the outcome and, we believe it is going to enhance our economy." Then they're fine. It's not going to work, I mean, all the time.

Julie Ann: Sometimes things don't work and sometimes you don't know until you try it.

Garry: Right. I'm just amazed that the number one baseball hitter in the world probably hits no more than a third of every ball that's thrown at him so...

Julie Ann: Right. People don't realize that. And he doesn't consider himself a failure and neither does anyone else.

Garry: Exactly, exactly.

Julie Ann: When I do work in change management, I emphasize that once you implement whatever that change is going to be, that's not the end. That's a new beginning. That's when it's time to realize you made all these plans and you think everything is going to work a certain way. Now, you have to look with fresh eyes to see if it is. Do we have tweaks to make?

Garry: Absolutely.

Julie Ann: Is this really a good idea? Good companies create products that don't work.

Garry: Well, I wouldn't be sitting here today if WD-40 had stopped at their first try. WD-40 is called WD-40 because there were 39 formulas that didn't work.

Julie Ann: I didn't know that.

Garry: If they stopped at 39, we wouldn't be having this conversation.

Julie Ann: Excellent.

Garry: The product was developed to stop corrosion in the umbilical cord of the Atlas Space Rocket. The chemist at the time, the company was called Robert Chemical Company, mixed up formulas. 39 of them didn't work and the 40th one did. It's called WD, which stands for, Water Displacement 40th Formula.

Julie Ann: Wow, I just learned a very good piece of Trivial Pursuit information.

Garry: That could win you a good glass of adult beverage if you care to partake in one of those dinner parties.

Julie Ann: That's excellent, thank you for sharing. See, I always get these bonuses on the show. I love too that you talked about allowing your people to grow. I think it's important for leaders to give people a space to grow. Back to having a safe space, sometimes they're going to grow in areas, and sometimes falter in others. They need support to grow. I'm sure you've had people come into your company that don't really fit the position they may have come in on, but they're a great addition to the entire workforce. So instead of letting them go, you find another space where they may fit better.

Garry: Absolutely. That's why our promise to our tribe members is we're not here to mark your paper, we're here to help you get an A. Back when I did my master's degree in leadership, we studied the leadership and development techniques that Jack Welsh used at GE. Their goal was to cull out the bottom 10% and I said, "Wait a minute. What if we actually dedicated ourselves to developing the bottom 10%?" If our organization had a goal of culling out the bottom 10%, I'd have to set a goal in our human resources department to hire their quota of losers that year. I don't want to do that.

Garry: My friend Whitney Johnson just wrote a new book called Building an A Team. She calls it the S curve. The S curve is a percentage of your people who are in the development stage. There's a percentage that are on that curve where they're accelerating. Then, the top end are those that are in the advanced stage. And it's so true. You're always going to have people at one stage of development in the organization. If we're truly committed to helping people get an A and creating an environment where they step into the best version of their personal self, our job as leaders and coaches is to help people get there. We call our bosses in the company coaches. That's one of the things that helps us retain people like millennials because they just want to continually learn and develop.

Julie Ann: Yes, they do.

Garry: We are a learning organization. We're continually evolving people with new projects, and new tasks to help them. Remember what I said in the beginning? Imagine a place where you go to work every day. You make a contribution to something bigger than yourself. You learn, have fun, and go home happy.

Julie Ann: And they're home life is better and so they come to work better. And so it goes. Everything is related. It's important to have that. I always say, "I help companies build a culture where people want to come to work, instead of going to the movies."

Garry: Certainly. And we know there's evidence, medical research out there that shows good work environments create an emotional presence in people where there's less chance in getting cancer, blah, blah, blah.

Julie Ann: Absolutely.

Garry: They go home happy, which makes their home lives better. I often say, "Great companies can enrich people who build great families, who build great communities, who can build great countries."

Julie Ann: Another part of my secret life is that I'm a certified laughter leader. I've learned a lot about laughter and how it changes you physically. Being happier with your life, of course, is connected with that. There are many, many studies about how your immune system is increased. Absolutely, when you have a workforce that is feeling good about what they're doing, who they're doing it for, and themselves, they tend to have less sick days.

Garry: I get goosebumps when I go into some of our operations and people say, "I loved coming to work today. It was exciting. I learned something. I had fun. I can't wait to go home and tell my family what I learned and how much fun I had."

Julie Ann: I know, that's kind of how I feel about WD-40.

Garry: Thank you.

Julie Ann: I'm going to make another assumption, and that is you have very low turnover.

Garry: Oh, yeah. We do. Our retention rate is five or six times that of the average in the US. Very long tenure, a lot of our people have been at the company 20 or 30 years. So yes, we value those tribe members. So retention is an economic plus and we have a great employer brand. People want to come and work for us. So even in times when there's a shortage of good people, we have people who love to think they can be part of a tribe where we care about them, and we're candid with them, and respect them. And they have fun and they do good work.

Julie Ann: It's interesting because I have tried many times to get companies to understand that having that kind of culture where people want to come to work also affords them getting other good employees because of the company's reputation. There are companies that actually use the podcast they do with me as part of their process for hiring people. This gives them a glimpse of what they're getting themselves into. They can reflect, and ask themselves, is this some place they want to be? For some people, it might not be a good fit. And you and I know time-wise and money-wise, it's a lot better to find out right away. That's why Tony Hsieh at Zappos pays people to leave after 30 days because it's cheaper, and a lot easier, and less disruptive with the rest of the workforce.

Garry: Totally.

Julie Ann: You don't want a black hole in the middle of your workforce.

Garry: I totally agree with you.

Julie Ann: Well, I'm pretty sure I could talk to you for another hour and a half, probably two days, but I think you have other things to do. You've given us some great ideas that our listeners can actually take out into their workforce and utilize for themselves. But if I'm finally convinced business culture is a good idea, what do you tell them to do as a first step? Because as far as I know, you have this down to a science, including the fact that you can make mistakes and get better. I commend you on that because I think it's part of the process. What would you say would be their first step?

Garry: To get comfortable with leadership is not about being in charge. Leadership is about taking care of those in your charge.

Julie Ann: Oh, I love it. Thank you so much Garry for being with us today. I really appreciate it and I'm sure my listeners do too.

Garry: My pleasure.

Favorite Food: Italian

If you are just reading this review section, go back. This man, this organization, is the epitome of a business that cares. Garry Ridge has all the elements that create a great leader and culture that I talked about in the first chapter. He knows how to listen and understands the value of a new idea. Seriously, this whole company was built on the necessity of having a continuous stream of new formulas or there would be no WD-40 company. What a wonderful underlying story to recreate every day. Continuous learning is mandatory for himself and his workforce. He is acutely aware of how that creates the greatest potential for each individual, including himself. Garry's humility is to be admired. Humility goes hand in hand with vulnerability. One aspect that companies tend to want, but not establish, is a safe environment. Everyone, of course, wants to be safe physically, but the company who can create an atmosphere where the workforce feels safe to speak up is a life long journey. WD-40 deliberately designs their culture this way because they understand and value the effect on the company's growth and success. There is no other way to say it. WD-40 is a force not to be reckoned with, but to admire and emulate.

Here are WD-40's company values:

» We value doing the right thing.

» We value creating positive, lasting memories in all our relationships.

» We value making it better than it is today.

» We value succeeding as a tribe while excelling as individuals.

» We value owning it and passionately acting on it.

» We value sustaining the WD-40 Company economy.

THE POWER OF PEOPLE FIRST

WITH JANICE MAZZALLO, CHRO, PEOPLESBANK

"Be absolutely transparent in sharing the results of your employee survey, good bad or otherwise."

Janice Mazzallo

I AM CONSTANTLY ON THE LOOKOUT for guests for my podcast, Businesses that Care. I read about a relatively small bank called, PeoplesBank, for six years in a row they won the award for the top place to work from the Boston Globe. That peaked my interest. In this gender lopsided world of executives, I am always eager to talk to women whose leadership has made successful strides in a business setting, and how they did it. The high-performance culture of PeoplesBank has made it the largest community bank in its market.

It wasn't easy to get on Janice's calendar, 8 months to be exact, but well worth it.

Janice's secrets, like so many in this book, stem from connecting with people on an emotional level, with recognition of value and the desire to see her workforce grow. All tied up with the idea that work can be fun.

Key to this episode was Janice's astute revelation that what happens with a person from the moment the acceptance letter is signed has long lasting results. PeoplesBank is acutely aware the first few months are critical in the longevity of an employee.

Conversation with Julie Ann and Janice:

Julie Ann: Janice Mazzallo has more than 25 years of human resource management experience and joined PeoplesBank in 2005. Now she's the Executive Vice President and Chief Human Resources Officer. During her tenure at the bank, she helped plan and implement a cultural shift to improve employee engagement, the impact on the community and overall performance of the organization. No surprise, I wanted her on Businesses That Care. Thank you so much for being with us today.

Janice: Good Morning, Julie Ann. Thank you so much. I'm so thrilled to be a part of this.

Julie Ann: I want to start out with you talking about this culture shift. I know you can't tell me how you did that in a half hour, but what I want to know is what sparked you to even think, maybe this is a good idea. Because there's a lot of people out there still thinking about whether this is important.

Janice: I will tell you, it was a journey. It started with the previous CEO who has since retired, who's actually on our board of directors. He and I shared the same vision and that was 14 years ago. We had both read the book, Good to Great by Jim Collins. After reading that book, we were inspired by the idea that if you put people first, it can really transform an organization. I think traditionally your typical bank tends to be more conservative, top-down. Certainly, in this organization 14 years ago, that's kind of where we were. He and I shared the vision that we wanted to create an environment where we put people first. We created a place where, not only did we want to focus on profitability, but we wanted people to do the right thing and have fun in the work environment. We looked to create a work environment where people felt empowered and they would have an opportunity for career development. We changed the paradigm and instead of saying it was about customers first, we focused on the people. Then, ultimately, the customer satisfaction would come.

Julie Ann: That's what the research shows us now. When people are happier at work, then their customers are happier with the service they get. It seems so obvious, but we have been living in this environment where the focus is only on customer experience. But we're now just realizing the root of that comes from the employee experience.

Janice: Absolutely. I can tell you now, 14 years later, as our levels of engagement have risen, so have our levels of profitability. It is amazing. In the last six years PeoplesBank has had the best years in terms of profitability.

Julie Ann: I'm a business culture consultant and I go in and explain to people, this takes time, it's a journey and your bottom line is going to change, but it's not going to be next week. I know it's all relative, but when did you really see that difference in profitability and a rise in customer satisfaction? I know you can't say it'll happen in four weeks, but can you give a range?

Janice: That's a very important piece. I want to mention a couple of things about that. First, it does take time and it does take patience. I think that's one of the missteps a lot of organizations make is that they think it's a one and done and that you can Band-Aid with some program du jour and that's going to fix everything. One of the things I really admired about the CEO I was working for is that he really got it. He understood that this was a journey and it was going to take time.

I had known from my career in human resources that, on average, to shift the culture it takes about seven years. So it took us probably a good three years before we started to really start to see change because we were a very traditional, conservative organization. The first thing we did was conduct an employee survey to really get a pulse for how people were feeling. My message to the CEO was if we're going to do that, we have to be absolutely transparent in sharing what the results are. Good or bad.

Julie Ann: That is a key piece to the process. Not only are you asking for their input, you are willing to share the results as well.

Janice: Yes.

Julie Ann: That creates buy-in in the beginning that motivates people to participate and be more honest, don't you think?

Janice: Yes, it does. It was incredibly eye opening to us because it really brought to light some of the major issues that we, quite frankly, knew about and some of them we didn't know about. Some of them we were going to be able to fix immediately and others were going to take some time. So that was sort of the baseline that we were dealing with.

Julie Ann: I think it's important to mention, to give you full credit, that when you're taking off on this journey and you're getting feedback, you also have to be the kind of leader that is open to what you weren't aware of in your organization. You aren't ignoring what is brought to your attention and only working on what you already knew about. It's such a process when you're having this cultural shift. It's more than just getting information, it's about your own openness and perspective. One of the things

I found across the board with the Businesses That Care podcast is great leadership is open to new ideas and new perspectives and new solutions.

Janice: Yes, absolutely. One of the things we discovered immediately is that our associates really didn't understand the direction of the organization. They didn't understand our vision or what we were trying to accomplish. More importantly, what their role was in the organization. So one of the first things we set out to do was to communicate the vision of the organization.

I was new to the organization, we had a new CEO and we also had a couple of other new senior management leaders. As a senior team we were creating a very new organization. Myself and a couple of senior management leaders, literally did a roadshow. We went out to the entire organization and talked in very simple terms of what we were trying to accomplish and what role each associate played in that. As you know communication is key. We took every opportunity to continue to reinforce that in every form of communication whenever we could to bring that up so that employees really understood that.

Julie Ann: I like that you called it a roadshow.

Because that's really what it is, right? In so many companies now, they have remote offices or they can't fit everyone in the same room so it's important to have that kind of communication. I do work with companies to create internal podcasts to get clear, concise and consistent messaging out to everyone.

Janice: What makes the story of PeoplesBank so great is that we're a relatively small organization to receive the designation of a Boston Globe top place to work for the last six years. We are a $2.5 billion asset bank, which in the banking world is relatively small and a 300-employee organization. It has been a great story to tell that we've been able to achieve this.

Julie Ann: One of the reasons you've been able to achieve this is your ability to get people engaged before they ever walk in the door. Talk about what you do from the time they look at a job ad, because now, employee engagement is becoming the employee experience, which is when I look at your ad, to when I walk out your door.

Janice: Absolutely. I am in an area in Western Massachusetts, they call it the Five College area, I am competing with lots of other employers for talent. We do a lot of recruiting of college students for a management development program. When my recruiter on the team goes out to job fairs or campus recruitment, she's competing with folks that are looking for students and can offer positions that have beer in the fridge and all kinds of fun things. Let's face it, banking is not exactly the sexiest type of job and career out there. I look at what is it that we have here at PeoplesBank that's going to resonate with potential college students out there? We really offer our culture. What we've got is something special that I think no one else has out there. I try to make an emotional connection immediately with people, including potential candidates and obviously with our associates. We do that through our social media and the many ways in which we do our recruitment. One of the unique things that we do in our onboarding process, is immediately after hiring candidates, we change our one-day orientation program into an onboarding program, which a lot of employers had done. In trying to make that emotional connection, we thought, why not send a message immediately upon that person accepting the offer. The message we want to send to them is how they are welcome to PeoplesBank. So, when Julie Ann accepts an offer at PeoplesBank, we immediately send an Edible Arrangement to their home saying, "Welcome to PeoplesBank, we're so happy you have joined this organization."

Julie Ann: Okay, I'm all excited. I got a job at PeoplesBank. I got my Edible Arrangement. I'm going to say it's a small idea, but it's a big idea, right?

Janice: Exactly.

Julie Ann: It doesn't cost you a lot of money.

Janice: It doesn't.

Julie Ann: I'm a big believer in simple solutions, big results, so what are some of the big results that you get from that?

Janice: I have to tell you, Julie Ann, it's probably one of the smallest ideas that has had the biggest impact, It's the personal touch, I think, that people love. It's that unexpected moment. What it also does is sends a message that we're not just welcoming the new associate to the bank. It's also their extended family or friends or whomever is living in their household because we're a community bank, we are a mutual bank, we're not a stock bank. We do a lot of community work and have a lot of social gatherings here at the bank and that's a really important part of our culture. So, it's important to send a message that we're not only welcoming the associate, but the people around them too.

Janice: When the person comes in, they always talk about how they barely got part of the fruit because their whole family wanted some of it. It's always a great hit. However, it's just a message, again of their value and a little bit of a warm touch on who we are and, a great way to start.

Julie Ann: You are letting them know that they are valued before they ever walked in the door.

Janice: Exactly.

Julie Ann: That has to build engagement.

Janice: The stats tell us that 69% of employees are likely to stay with a company for several years if they experience a great onboarding process. It makes good business sense too. It's not just a feel-good thing. From a business perspective, it makes good business sense to have a great onboarding program. We also assign every new hire to what we call a buddy. Liken it to your first day of school. Who can't relate to that nervousness on your first day of work?

Julie Ann: A must in culture building is that somebody has, not only a buddy on the first day, but someone they can go to any time if they have a question about a process or a procedure or a software they're using.

Janice: Exactly. We have that person reach out to them, even before they start. They call them before they join the bank and say, "Hey, I'm your buddy and I can't wait for you to start." They plan to have lunch with them on the first day so the new hire knows they won't be stuck down in the cafeteria by themselves.

Julie Ann: It re-engages the person reaching out too.

Janice: Exactly. Yes. We choose those buddies very carefully and we make sure that the people that are selected are highly engaged. We try to match them up with the new associate personality-wise too.

Julie Ann:	Great idea. What else do you do with onboarding that makes people so excited about coming in your door?
Janice:	At their three-month mark we have a breakfast with all of the senior leaders and all of our new hires. We come together as a group and then we talk strategy.
Julie Ann:	They probably all think they're going to get fired.
Janice:	Actually they love it. We try to keep it light and fun in line with our culture. We do a great icebreaker where we do this fun sort of non-business questions in the morning. And even the senior officers participate.
Julie Ann:	Great.
Janice:	Then, every senior officer will talk about their division and what the strategic objectives are coming up for the year. It gives the new hires an opportunity to talk to the President of the bank and all of the senior leaders. We just had one about a week ago and we get an incredible amount of questions and interaction. People feel very comfortable talking. It's a wonderful opportunity to have that kind of access to senior leaders.
Julie Ann:	Back to research. When people feel connected to senior leadership they have a different work ethic. Their work has a different quality. They're more in tune with the purpose of the organization, which also changes the work they produce or even the ideas that they come up with. They become better problem solvers and it really changes the whole dynamic of an organization when people feel connected to leadership.
Janice:	Right. And to give credit to the current CEO, who took over a couple of years ago, he has continued to support the culture. He makes it a point when he meets with our new hires, emphasize the importance of the culture and how

important the associates are in supporting our customers. They are everything when it comes to the importance of customer interaction and ultimately the profitability of the bank.

Julie Ann: There are always people out there who maybe haven't started this process yet. The last book I wrote, Blueprint for Employee Engagement, was about 37 essential ways to break it down. People think, "Employee engagement! It's just too big." They know it's going to take a lot of time and they know they have to be persistent. The change looks too big so nobody takes a step. So that was the idea of the book, that here are 37 little steps you can take, just take one.

Implement one idea. If you could go back in time, none of these things are in place, and you start over, what's your first step? What's your first suggestion for a first step?

Janice: Hands down, without a doubt, conduct an employee survey.

Julie Ann: And did you do that yourself?

Janice: We used an outside firm and I would highly recommend that. I believe it's important because employees want to know that their opinions and their input is confidential.

Julie Ann: And anonymous.

Janice: Yes. I think it's important to assure them of that.

Julie Ann: I do too. How did you find a firm with so many out there?

Janice: There are many, many out there. I did some research through the different bank associations. That's how I found the current one that we're using and have been using. It's called Energage. They are a national firm and

I'll put a shout out to them. I would highly recommend them. The second piece of that is if you're going to survey your associates it is critical that you share the information, as I mentioned earlier.

Julie Ann: The good, the bad and the ugly.

Janice: Yes, regardless of what the results are and you should follow up on those results.

Julie Ann: That's a biggie right there. However, that's the whole idea of this cultural shift is it isn't a one and done. You don't have somebody come in and do a motivational speech and leave.

You might motivate one person in that room for several weeks. But you need to build this within the fabric of the company.

Janice: Absolutely.

Julie Ann: Janice thanks so much for sharing your experience with our audience. I really appreciate it and they do too, another great perspective on how to create that cultural shift.

Janice: Thank you so much. I really appreciate you doing this for the audience. I think it's just a great resource and thank you so much for the opportunity Julie Ann.

Favorite Food: Eggplant Parmesan

I like the statistic that 69% of workers will stay a few years longer if they have a good onboarding experience. First impressions are not only for the job seeker. In fact, our current situation creates an environment where the first impression is just as important for the employer. People are looking at your website and making decisions if they want to apply. In the same way they use Yelp to decide where they want to eat, they also look at Glassdoor to see where they want to work. Janice has created an onboarding process that starts before an individual starts their first day of work. A small gift and a call from their buddy, creates a bond to the organization immediately.

Change can only occur long term with the support of the entire leadership team. As you have seen in other chapters, increased visibility of leadership forms a community, as opposed to a hierarchy. Your workforce will perform at higher levels when they truly feel a part of a team effort, when they understand the strategic plan of the organization, and when leadership is available and forthcoming.

Nobody ever said it was going to be easy. Our world is filled with fast solutions, but building a culture that allows you to recruit and retain great talent doesn't happen quickly. Be patient, be open, and be willing to try something new. The results might amaze you.

SETTING A WORLD EXAMPLE

WITH EMILY M. DICKENS, CHIEF OF STAFF, SHRM

" The organization itself has to be flexible with its people by providing opportunities for growth."

Emily M. Dickens

IT'S NOT EASY HAVING THE WORLD watching you. SHRM, the Society for Human Resource Management is the world's largest HR professional society, representing 300,000 members in more than 165 countries. It's important for them to be an example of what they stand for. There is a lot changing inside their walls, with a fairly new CEO and lots of new ideas. Their changes affect their membership, the community and their internal workforce.

Emily M. Dickens has an energy about her that draws you in. Her goal is to make sure that each employee at SHRM is aware of the opportunities available so that more people will take advantage of them. She wants to give each employee the tools and skills they need to perform at their highest level. Maybe because she is an attorney, communication is of the upmost importance to her. At SHRM people are encouraged to move from their current position if it no longer serves them. Emily knows, if it's not a good fit, that effects the entire organization and the individual's well-being. What she wants is for each team member to be excited about how they contribute to the goals of the Society. She knows to get there; you have to work from the top down.

CONVERSATION WITH JULIE ANN AND EMILY:

Julie Ann: I had the privilege of speaking at the SHRM Talent Management Conference. While I was there, they introduced the SHRM Chief Human Resources Officer and chief of staff, Emily M. Dickens. Her beauty, her smarts, and how well she articulated her message struck me. She's an attorney with experience in government, higher education, and the non-profit sector. Now, she is the human resource face of SHRM, the society for human resource management. Which is a society across the world, that's a huge responsibility. I'm curious what that's like, but today, we're going to focus on what the working environment is like inside of this important, professional society with over 285,000 members in over 165 countries. Whew, that is big.

Julie Ann: Welcome to our podcast Emily, thanks so much for being here.

Emily: Thanks so much for having me, it's an honor.

Julie Ann: So you haven't been in this job that long.

Emily: No, my goodness, it's been a long nine and a half months. And actually, I'm wearing a number of hats, as you mentioned, but I want to make sure I say I am interim CHRO because I know that many of our SHRM members out there are looking forward to us putting someone permanently in that position. I know so many of them think they're the person and so hope is still alive.

Julie Ann: Are you getting a lot of bribes, a lot of candy and flowers?

Emily: Oh my gosh, I met people everywhere; I've picked up resumes everywhere I go. The great thing is, we knew this was something that was so important that Johnny, as frugal as he is, agreed to hire an outside firm to find the next SHRM CHRO. But I tell you, while I'm here in the interim, I'm having a lot of fun, I've been doing this part of the job since May. But joined Johnny here in January.

Julie Ann: Let's tell people you're talking about Johnny C. Taylor, who's the new CEO of SHRM.

Emily: Yes, that's right. So, I'll say that I've been having a fun time doing this since May, as the interim CHRO, but I was honored to join SHRM is January when Johnny C. Taylor Jr. took over as the new CEO. Johnny was no stranger to SHRM, he was a former board chairman. He's been a CHRO in the corporate arena, and a big supporter of the organization. And he was formally the CEO of Thurgood Marshall College Fund, where I was his general counsel. It's an honor to come here and not be general counsel. Instead, I get to focus on some other things while I'm here as chief of staff, and of course, in this role.

Julie Ann: So let's talk about that a little bit because I mean SHRM's whole purpose is to assist and support and give great information and ideas to the people out in the world who are running and working in the human resources department. So those are some big shoes to fill and I'm sure there are plenty of them out there like me and even people who aren't in human resources that want to know what are you doing inside SHRM? What's your culture like? What's your employee engagement? What's it like inside those walls?

Emily: Wow, it's a lot of pressure, I'll tell you. One of the things our CEO said early on is that SHRM's HR should be the example for all HR.

Julie Ann: Exactly.

Emily: Which means we have to be courageous, have to take risks, and we have to be innovative. And that all fell in line with something we started the first 30 days here. And the first 30 days of Johnny's new administration, the executive team got together and did a couple of things. One of which was to review our value system, which is what we call Guiding Principles. The executive team came up with five guiding principles, which will guide our culture and the culture we want to be, because it's a transition to transformation. We're transforming the organization into its next iteration and you needed the proper culture to do that.

   We literally dedicated three of our executive team meetings to talk about what that culture would look like. It was an exercise. Some of you may know, Alex Alonso, our Chief Knowledge Officer here. He's brilliant. He sat in the room with all of us and we threw out our ideas of what we think a good culture looks like, and what words describe a great culture. Alex put that all together and we came up with our five guiding principles. So, when we talk about what type of person and what type of environment we want to have here at SHRM, we say, "We want people who want to lead with a bold purpose. People who believe in excellence and accountability, who are agile and flexible, smart and curious, and open collaborators." That's the type of person we're looking for.

Julie Ann: Nice.

Emily: We believe that if our culture really focuses around those five things, we get people who believe in those five things, who live it and work it, that we'll have the culture that SHRM needs to be the standard for the greatest HR association in the world. It's been a lot of work doing that.

Julie Ann: I'm sure it has. But one of the ideas you mentioned that I think is really necessary is to be bold as well as curious. I interviewed a CEO not too long ago and he said, "If you don't have ideas that don't work, then you don't have enough ideas." And that's part of being bold you have to try things. I remind my clients this isn't in stone, let's work on this for six months. It doesn't mean it's the end of it, we may have to tweak it, we may have to throw it out, who knows? But until you try, you don't know. I interviewed the CEO of WD-40 and I didn't realize at the time, they base their whole culture on coming up with ideas that don't work or they wouldn't even have a company. Because that 40 stands for 40 formulas. They had 39 formulas that failed before it worked.

Emily: You're right. We talk about failing fast. If you don't give people in the room to innovate, to try something, then how do you promote a culture that's flexible and bold, you know? So, for us, it's really if you have an idea, you've been working in this arena for 10, 20 years, if there's something you see that doesn't work and you think you have an answer, why shouldn't you feel like you should try it out? That's what we want people to do. You know, HR, just like everything else, is changing every day. We can't be stagnant. We have to be looking around the corner at all times to see what we can find or discover that will best serve our members and the HR profession as a whole. And being innovating, being flexible, being bold and saying, "We've never tried this before," do you think someone would've thought 10, 20 years ago that we would have 17,000 people at our annual conference and that we would figure out how to accommodate them and make it an experience for all of them?

Julie Ann: Yes that was jaw dropping for me.

Emily: Yes, and so even if we look at what other things we offer here and ways to support the HR profession, we're trying to be bold in all our actions internally and externally.

Julie Ann: Can you talk about a couple of particular ideas that you are implementing now and maybe where they come from, and how they're working and changing the internal culture of SHRM?

Emily: We have this thing here, I guess people would call it an all-hands meeting, all staff meeting, and we call it Star Coffee. It's one of the first things I was introduced to about SHRM. I joined Johnny at Star Coffee before we started here, just to kind of see where everything was here. I remember turning around and seeing all these people in a really tight room standing around trying to hear the message that Hank was giving, that's the former CEO. I was thinking, "Oh, we have to find another place to host these meetings when we get here." Because how often do you get the majority of the staff in one room? And they were doing it about five or six times a year. We're going to do it about four times a year, but really, this is our opportunity to get the staff excited about SHRM, the business of SHRM, and what we're doing. Now, every Star Coffee has been offsite because we needed space to accommodate all of our employees. At least two of them are mandatory because we have a number of remote employees. You hear that they don't feel engaged, but at least once or twice a year they come to the home office for meetings with their department. We schedule them, we tell them in advance when the event is going to be, so the departments can hold those meetings around the time we're hosting Star Coffee. I walked into the last one, we hosted it at a local community college, and someone said to me, "It reminded me of one of those Walmart shareholder meetings because there were lights, camera, action." We had music playing and videos on the screen that were playing as people were coming in.

Julie Ann: You were having an event.

Emily: We plan a lot of events for our members, but how many events do we plan for our people? We love the annual picnic people love that, right? But why not put on an event where our people get excited about it? Since then we've held it in a movie theater and gave everybody movie tickets right after. We can do fun things, but also do important things. Like enforcing our culture. So, every Star Coffee, we pick one of the guiding principles to focus on. The most recent one was being agile and flexible. And I tell you, our Executive Director of our foundation, Wendi Safstrom, got up there and put on just the most amazing presentation about what it means to be agile and flexible. It was funny, it was quirky, and it resonated with everyone in the room. That's what we want to do. We want to spend time talking about those things that are important to our culture. At that event we also recognize new hires, we do something called, The People Parade for those who have been promoted. They get to cross the stage with music. People are going to tell you it's the best part about being in HR now, is when people get promoted. I love that, especially internal folk. Think about all these people who have been here for years who found an opportunity to elevate themselves and therefore, elevate SHRM. It's amazing. So we do the People Parade, and then we ask all the new hires to stand. We had 39 new hires in between the last two Star Coffees.

Julie Ann: Wow.

Emily: It was amazing. We had them all sit together. It was the first group, all shapes, sizes, colors, and from all sorts of different environments. It made us so proud. And that's the type of thing you can do no matter what your budget is. Everybody has a different budget, right?

Julie Ann: Exactly.

Emily: As we do the budgeting process for this year, we've decided that those events are important. We're going to do it at least four times a year and we're going to make it an event so our staff understands that we're putting that event on for them. We want them to be impressed with us and where we're going.

Julie Ann: I am a big advocate that we don't celebrate enough in organizations. This is a great idea. Sometimes we only celebrate at the end of a project. Why not celebrate a new hire when you're bringing somebody into the family? For that person whose just been hired into SHRM, they're thinking to themselves, that they made the right decision. Because sometimes it's hard to come into a company, whether it is big or small, really doesn't matter. Sometimes it's more difficult when it's smaller. It's hard to fit into the "family." So, what you're doing is you're opening up your arms and saying, "We are celebrating that you're here. We want to bring you into the fold. We want to celebrate the people who have elevated themselves through hard work and have fun and work hard." And I think those two can go well together.

Emily: I agree, even if it's something small that people don't think about a lot. When I arrived on my first day, I looked at my desk and I said, "Where's my gift?" And everybody laughed at me, and I said, "No, no, no. I had an expectation," because I'd worked somewhere else and on your first day you get a shirt. You got a nice pullover that had the organization's logo on it. And I really believed that the first day when you walk to your desk, you should never walk to an empty desk. So, now, again, you have to figure out how to allocate the resources, but I think it's a priority, I think it's something important, so your first day you show up in your office or your cubicle, there's a bag with your name on it and it has lots of little SHRM goodies. On your first day you know you're a part of us and you have something to show for it. I know it's not a lot, pens, paper, you know?

Julie Ann: Doesn't matter.

Emily: I just think that first gift on the first day says, "We want you here, you're welcomed here. And we want you to be a part of the family, here's your uniform." My next idea is I think everybody here should have polo shirts. It's the little stuff, right? Not cheap polos, but nice polo shirts that at least everyone here has one because if you think about it, we hired 39 people between two quarters, they won't have it. They wouldn't have attended an outside event or had the opportunity to purchase it; we don't have an onsite store. Just little things so people can feel like they're part of a family.

Julie Ann: Yes, which is huge. Now, you talked about the five guiding principles, which we will put in the show notes so everybody can see exactly what they are. Pick another guiding principle, if you will, and let us know what you're doing inside your environment. It's interesting, you know, a lot of people have vision statements and mission statements and core values, but if they don't live them somehow within the organization, they become meaningless. And the people who are working there, they really become meaningless to them, because they say, "Oh yes, they have it on the wall, but they don't do anything." What I'm hearing you say is that you are taking those guiding principles and saying, "No, we are going to take specific initiatives to live each of these." So do you have another one you'd like to share? Maybe something that's going on inside SHRM?

Emily: Well how about, I like stretch assignments, I don't know about you, but I've been able to learn so much from stretch assignments and actually leverage them into the next position.

Julie Ann: What does that mean to you, stretch assignment?

Emily: To me it is some assignment that is outside of your department or division and usually outside of the scope of work that you typically do here. I'll give you an example; we had an Executive Assistant (EA) who was in one division. We're bringing in a new chief and I didn't have an EA for her yet, but I wanted her to have support. So, I asked this other executive assistant whether she would support both people at one time. That was really outside what she had been doing in one division for a decade or so. This new division was a brand-new division and we needed somebody to help that chief from the ground up. We use the chief model here. She did so amazing that that chief wanted to hire her as her EA, right? Because it was a totally different division, what it did was expose her to another area of the organization that she could use in her existing area to do her work. It was the same administration support, but it was a different level of support that was needed. This person needed lots of charts and research.

Julie Ann: Different language.

Emily: Yes. She needed research, and charts and presentations. Where the EA's other job was usually to help with scheduling and regular daily administrative issues. It allowed her to get some new skills and use those skills in her original position. That's what we mean when we talk about being flexible and agile. It was an opportunity for her to learn a new part of the business, so there was some smart and curious in there too. Being flexible, because now she was managing two executives, while understanding the value of having that extra experience. I sponsor the group of administrative assistants here, because I worked my way through law school with somebody's EA. So I feel very passionate about that group of employees, they're the foundation for us. And I want them to all be able to get different experiences so they understand how the business works together. Anytime I have an opportunity to do that, we try to do it.

Julie Ann: I think the key word there is opportunity. So you ask this person if they wanted that opportunity to expand. When they say yes, their skill set grows and who knows where that's going to help them within the organization. Sometimes what happens in business is people are in one department but excel in a different department. You don't know that until they get that opportunity. Maybe they should be in sales, instead of marketing, for instance, right?

Emily: You are so right. That means that the organization itself has to be flexible with its people by providing opportunities for growth. So even looking internally and making sure that HR is going to the people and saying, "Look, we have 35 openings now. If you are an internal person and you want to be considered and you don't know whether your skill set that you're using here can match up, please go talk to our new manager of talent." We are vocal with that. We do it in writing on our SHRM LinkedIn, we do it at the Star Coffee, every chance we get. Anytime I see someone I know that's been in the same position for a while, having those discussions with him or her and saying, "What do you want to do next? What do you think you could next? Do you think there's anything here?" I want to create opportunities for people to interview and talk to other departments. We have had a lot of movement that has been lateral and that's not a bad thing, when you're thinking about letting your people understand that importance of being flexible, agile, smart, and curious, right? Learning across the business. You never know how that's going to work for our business later on or for that person.

Julie Ann: It's a huge piece of employee engagement too. When you ask people if they want to learn something new, you are giving them a new opportunity. If they have been feeling stagnant because they have been doing the same job for 10 years, it can be an alternative to stay within the "family." The chance to be supported while doing something new is a boost for employee engagement. People feel cared for.

Emily: Yes, and I just had a young man in my office. It turns out that he went to my alma mater, a few years after I did, and I didn't know it. He told me he was going back to school to pick up some additional skills in IT. I said, "Well, did you go see our friend in HR that helps with our educational fund?" And he said, "No." And I said, "Why not?" I feel like our executive team have to be walking billboards for employee resources.

Julie Ann: I like that.

Emily: And not just human resources. Anytime we're having a conversation with someone, we should be like, "Well do you know about this benefit? Are you using this benefit? How is that benefit working for you? Have you heard about that?" We're offering these benefits and look, you talk about it once or twice a year and sometimes it's too much. It's all coming at you at once and all people really want to focus on is, "Do I have health benefits?" That's the most important thing. Can I get covered? Is it going up this year or not? And they're not thinking about the 401k management or the fact that we have a pension. They're not thinking about the educational benefits. What I say to the executive team a lot is, "You have to be walking billboards talking about what SHRM continues to offer." It doesn't get on people's nerves, but I think it's getting through to people and especially the executive team to ask these questions when you're having conversations. We have opportunities for people who have lunch with chiefs that are not their chief, so you get to meet another member of the executive team. During those meetings, executives should say, "What are your educational goals? Do you need help? Do you know we provide this? Are you somebody that likes to work out? Do you know we have a person that comes onsite and does workouts here twice a week?" Those types of things that people forget about because they're just going through their everyday business.

Emily: So if we're walking billboards, if we're the ones that are continuing to remind our people about the resources and benefits that we're providing for them and getting them to sign up for them, I think there's value there.

Julie Ann: You know, I'm having this vision in my head of you with a sandwich board on, but a very nice one. Walking up and down the halls going, "The workout people are coming on Tuesday." You know?

Emily: Whatever we have to do, right?

Julie Ann: We have about five minutes left. So, what I want to know is, what are you looking at for the future? What types of stretch goals do you have, if you will, for SHRM? We'll start with that. What's on your horizon? What do you have in this back corner of your brain? You probably have a hundred or a thousand. When I was saying that, it looked like you were thinking, "How am I going to pick one?"

Emily: Oh gosh. I'm going to tell you one thing that's really important. Our last CHRO, did an amazing job. She convinced the organization that we needed to invest in something called SHRMU. It is an ongoing series of course offerings that vary. There are sessions about culture, classes that help you do your job better. They're taught by in-house SHRM experts and by SHRM members who come in and teach the courses for us. We're really trying to expand that and also trying to make some of those courses mandatory. We do a great course here called, The Business of SHRM. We've decided that every new employee needs to see that because you need to understand where you fit in the whole picture. I think a lot of people get hired sometimes and it's very easy to get in your office and your cubicle and say, "Here's my job description, here's what I'm supposed to do and that's it." But you're not realizing how it works across the organization. I took it, even being eight months into the organization. I was like, "Oh I know everything, and I've been studying." I came to the class and there was still stuff that I was able to learn about just how our business connects across all the divisions. So, we've decided that it'll be important for every new person here to make sure they understand where they fit and where there are opportunities for them from the outset. We think that's important. We want to expand the offerings. We understand that SHRMU is really our organizational learning and development arm. We're coming up with the topics we need to do the business of SHRM, how to be the best independent contributor you can be, and how to be the best manager you can be. We're really working and focusing on that. So the sooner I can hire an employment engagement manager, the sooner that Edward Yost and I, whose going to be the person in charge of SHRMU, can really flush out all the amazing ideas we have about making that a prime example of what other organizations can do to help train their people internally.

Julie Ann: And how is SHRMU being put out? Are they onsite presentations? Are they podcasts?

Emily: So, not podcasts yet, we're getting there. We'll start out mostly as onsite presentations, but you know, space is limited. And there's demand, and we only have a few conferences to do it. So now, we started videotaping many of the presentations, including the business of SHRM because we couldn't keep up with demand. And the person that teaches that course is actually our chief global development officer. He's got a real day job, he can't teach us all the time. We literally just videoed his last class so that we can now use that. We can send the video to anybody who we've newly hired in that period, between when they signed the offer letter and the time they start. They can watch it, and they come in there the first day with some perception of where they fit in. Then, we're also going to be doing more webinars because we have a number of remote employees. It's mandatory to have a number of these classes during the year. So, we do webinars so they're able to get in there. Podcasts might be a good idea, but I have to think about that one.

Julie Ann: All right, so I'm an executive out there, I've heard your great ideas. Unfortunately, there are still a lot of businesses out there that just feel like employee engagement and business culture is too big to tackle. And you're standing in front of them and saying, "Here's your first step," what would that be?

Emily: Wow. Your first step is being transparent with yourself and your leadership team about what you want this organization to be. It's not about just how much money you want the organization to be able to clear at the end of the year. It's what type of feeling do you get when you walk through the door? What type of people do you want to be surrounded with? Who do you want to create with? I think if you start there, you develop a culture that won't have a lot of bad actors. You will have people who are transparent when there are issues and who will be honest with you about those issues. You'll have people who will always be looking to make the culture better.

Julie Ann: I love it. Emily, thank you so much for being with us today. I really appreciate it. It was great to kind of get inside this big, beautiful organization that I feel very much a part of and find out what's going on inside and what steps you're taking to be that shining example of what you want for your members.

Emily: Well thank you so much. And look, no one's perfect, you won't get it perfect. But we're going to keep failing fast and trying until we get it right.

Julie Ann: Thank you.

Favorite Food: Lasagna

Maybe it's because they are living with glass walls. To lead hundreds of thousands of people in HR best practices, you better be following your own advice. I am not sure which of their guiding principles I like best, but I can tell you this, SHRM is certainly living them. Their engagement in their staff's future exudes Flexibility and Agility in the development of the workforce and the organization. SHRM is open and vulnerable enough to offer new challenges and opportunities. They show that they are truly curious when they ask their employees, "What do you want?"

A part of their new flagship program, SHRMU, is focused on individuals knowing and understanding the organization's Bold Purpose. And although they want to have fun, Excellence and Accountability is required at all levels. SHRM wants their people to be SMART and they are willing to give them the tools and skills necessary to do that.

Giving, caring, asking for ideas, help and guidance, along with their guiding principles builds a foundation for their Collaborative Openness.

It's not easy being the world's example, but I think SHRM is up for the task when it comes to building a model culture. In the words of Emily M. Dickens, "No one's perfect, you won't get it perfect. But we're going to keep failing fast and trying until we get it right."

SHRM's Guiding Principles:

» Bold Purpose

» Excellence & Accountability

» Flexibility & Agility

» Smart & Curious

» Collaborative Openness

A HUGE Thank You!

NONE OF THIS WOULD BE possible without the amazing leaders I have had the privilege of interviewing. I appreciate their willingness to take time out of their busy day to share their success, openly and authentically.

Having just published a book last year, I had no intentions of doing it again in 2018. When Justin Sachs, from Motivational Press, reached out and encouraged me, I could not say no. Thank you, Justin, for believing in my idea and supporting me through this journey and, to your entire team for their dedication and patience.

A special thank you to a new friend, Simone Morris. Frankly speaking, without her encouragement, this book would not have been finished.

My professional speaking colleagues have been a vast sea of support, patience, great ideas and above all love. I feel blessed and forever grateful.

To my friend, mentor and sometimes cowboy, Jeffrey Hayzlett, thanks for writing my forward. You Rock!

To Joy, my four-legged friend, for all the times I made you wait to go for a walk, Good Dog!

Julie Ann Sullivan November 1, 2018

ABOUT THE AUTHOR

JULIE ANN SULLIVAN is a business culture expert who works with organizations that want to create a workplace where people are productive, engaged, and appreciated. She founded her company with the purpose of creating a more positive culture one person at a time.

Julie Ann earned a BA in psychology and an MBA in accounting. As a CPA, she spent decades in the financial industry and the corporate world. As a professional speaker and consultant, some of the companies she has worked with are McDonald's USA, Howard Hanna Financial, Highmark, and Bayer US.

She is host of the Mere Mortals Unite and Businesses that Care podcast, streaming around the world

Fun Facts:

Danced on American Bandstand

Spent 50th birthday in Machu Pichu

Is an Expert Level Certified Laughter Leader and Trainer

Contact Julie Ann Sullivan

(724) 942-0486

JulieAnn@JulieAnnSullivan.com

Learn more:

Website: JulieAnnSullivan.com

LinkedIn: Linkedin.com/in/JulieAnnSullivan

Twitter: JASatLNE

Facebook: Facebook.com/JulieAnnSullivanSpeaker

You Tube: Youtube.com/JulieAnnSullivan123